D1617120

Nudge Me Gently

"Everybody needs his memories.
They keep the wolf of
insignificance from the door."

Saul Bellow

Larry E. Perkinson

Nudge Me Gently

Special thanks to my wife Julie Ann and my sister Lynette Krueger for all their support and encouragement.

Happy 89th birthday to my father, Lester E. Perkinson, Sr. (June 25, 1926)

Congratulations to my parents on their 67th wedding anniversary (June 25, 1948). Dad chose a day he would not forget.

The cover picture is from the archives (or picture drawer) of Helen and Elza Stoner, my aunt and uncle.

Published June 15, 2015

CreateSpace Independent Publishing Platform

ISBN–13: 978-1512097023

ISBN–10: 1512097020

Forward: Nudge Me Gently

Scripture had been read, hymns sung, and quiet time was upon us. Seated on the pew in the back of the church, I felt safe. In my heart, I was snugly nestled in the hands of God and sheltered from harm's way. But the peaceful bliss ended abruptly when my wife's elbow plowed into my ribs. Apparently my snoring had interrupted her communion time.

When I lose my way like that and need to be reminded where I am and why I'm there, somebody or something generally rescues me. In silence Julie's harmless punch and puzzled glare had screamed, "What are you doing?" The elbow jab was more than justified, but it completely shattered my inner calmness.

Actually most days are poke free, and good intentions are often rewarded. On the last day of school, for example, breakfast for the grandchildren was meant to be a feast. The menu included smoked sausage and eggs and French toast slices that came fresh from the grocery's frozen aisle. Cereal was an option, and bacon was available if they wanted it.

The sausage was sliced into half-dollar, easy-to-swallow pieces as the stove heated up. Then I worked back and forth between the toaster and the frying pan. In between, the butter and syrup were placed on the table along with two glasses of milk.

When it was egg-fryin' time, some bacon grease was scooped into the pan. Admittedly, I looked both ways to see if anybody from the health clinic was writing a lard citation. Our busy schedule would not allow for that.

1

Surprisingly when I cracked the first egg into the skillet, I heard the echo of my mom at work: not Mom today, but that hero of yesteryear who could feed five, check our hair, tie our shoes, and smell if we had brushed our teeth ... all at the same time.

As soon as those eggs hit the hot surface, they sizzled and popped. Grease splattered toward my shirt and tie, but the damage was dodged. I am no culinary expert, but I don't believe that Teflon-cooking sprays create those same scintillating hisses.

For a moment I felt as comfortable as I had when I had dozed off during the church service. Cooking with the grease was the way my mother had fried food. I was listening to the breakfast of my youth and wondering when Mom would shoo me out of the kitchen until everything was ready. Again, I enjoyed the idea of someone taking care of me.

Colors and sounds and smells bring back vivid pictures and feelings. They can revive moments both great and small, moments that unveil comical recollections and moments that summon the presence of those we love. Sometimes the memories are aroused by such seemingly insignificant sources like the softness of a piece of fabric, the fragrance of fresh-baked biscuits, or the familiar words of an old song.

For me, recalling a time gone by has its benefits, so I enjoy reminiscing. On a bad day, when the positives are hard to find, an almost forgotten experience might just ease in unexpectedly and brighten my day or highlight what is really important in life.

Truthfully, none of us should wallow in the "yesterday was perfect" zone, but there is nothing wrong with reaching into the past for a little motivation and guidance. Purposeful reminders of life's lesson, tough or funny, can push us to a better place. Chance events can affect us. So can the wisdom of stories and our interaction with others.

And if a little encouragement or some food for thought is needed, try cooking with the bacon grease or falling asleep at the meetinghouse. You never know when you might get gently nudged in the right direction.

Nudge Me Gently

Nudge Me Gently

Towards Remembrance

Sister Linda hogging my tricycle seat

"When I was younger I could remember
anything, whether it happened or not; but
I am getting old, and soon I shall
remember only the latter."

Mark Twain, a Biography

The Fall

One of my earliest toys was a genuine, plastic flintlock pistol that Aunt Helen gave me. I kept it under my pillow for years. And there must have been a miniature bass drum before that. I dreamed of it when I was little. I could feel the straps on my shoulders and see my hands pounding the white surface with the wooden sticks.

But, the favorite pre-school possession was my first set of wheels. It was a new, metal tricycle, a man's machine. Solid rubber tires with white hubs and a fender over the front added a touch of class. There were no plastic parts and no tassels on the hand grips. Pedestrians envied the glossy, candy-apple red finish.

Our home was in Reddington, Indiana, and for a while that little place seemed very nearly perfect. It was a rural Eden with a fenced-in yard, a garden, and our own serpent in a tree. Obviously history repeats itself a lot.

No, the snake did not tempt to us or even get a chance to bother anyone, at least not more than once. Gene and I were playing under the tree when our sister spotted a black snake hanging from the limb above us. She went inside and tattled on the big worm.

It was immediately evident that worms were not welcome. After escorting us into the house with Linda, our mother fetched a hoe from the shed. We were not allowed to watch when she beat the daylights out of the intruder. Adam could have taken a lesson.

Another disruption to that peaceful community occurred when I went outside to play after a rain storm. I was ready to do some serious muddin' on the shiny trike, but my dependable ride had disappeared. Unlike today when my memory is questionable, I was completely in charge of my faculties at the age of four. I knew it was gone.

The search intensified, and eventually the three-wheeler was spotted. Next door a boy about my size was burning the tread off the tires as he pedaled like a demon all over his driveway. It still upsets me that a neighbor was showing off when I wanted to. Later I would find that my mother had let him borrow it. She definitely misjudged my willingness to share.

Intending to reclaim what was mine, I tried scaling the fence, but the wire was not stretched tightly enough. It sagged and swayed under my weight, and I could not keep my balance. So instead I grabbed hold of the wooden gate at the corner of the house and started to shinny up. Climbing came natural. When I was a baby, an elastic cord had been tied around my waist to keep me from going up and over the bars of the crib.

If it had not rained, I might have made it. Instead I slipped as I neared the top and was about to step over. It may not be of theological importance, but for me it was The Fall. My bike was still on the other side of the fence, but I was on the ground and in shock. When I fell, my leg caught against the guttering that came down the corner of the house. The curved drain spout sliced deeply into my left thigh. Blood dripped from the pipe that had funneled rain water an hour before.

Towels were thrown over the gaping wound, and I was placed in the backseat of the car. At the Columbus hospital, the doctor cleaned and numbed the wound. Then the nurses found the needle and thread. It tickled when my leg was sewn back together. Years later I counted fifty stitches, but I may have looked at the needle marks on each side of the scar.

I only wish that were the worst of it. The immediate care gave me hope. Bandages hid the damage, and the bleeding stopped. The attention I got at home confirmed that I really was mom's favorite, but the ordeal was not over. The real struggle started at the follow-up appointment.

When we returned to the hospital room that smelled of antiseptic alcohol, a courteous member of the nursing staff helped me up on the patient table. Initially everyone was so nice. It was fun to wiggle around on the padded top, but the social amenities ended when they told me to lie still while the embroidery work on my leg was examined.

The doctor unwrapped the dressing, swabbed the area, and reached for scissors. He explained that he was going to remove the thread and acted like I would be happy with his decision. Well, I wasn't born yesterday. If the stitches were pulled out, my thigh would split wide open again. I was sure of that.

I shrieked and lunged from the table, but the staff was pretty sneaky. It was apparent that others before me had challenged that procedure. Three or four more nurses were hiding in the hallway. Those ladies carried me in and held me down. It took all of them to do it, and there is a good chance that no one escaped an earache. My blood-curdling scream echoed throughout the building and into the parking lot. They were lucky that the injury did not reopen, or I would have yelled a lot louder.

It was a lesson that I have not forgotten. I departed less naive. If a mom would give away her son's tricycle and a bunch of nurses would fight a defenseless child, it was going to be a tough life. I planned to be better prepared for future conflicts.

Grace

My brothers Gene and Lester save me all the time. Basically, I have no understanding of motors, electrical wires, or plumbing, but they are walking, talking handyman encyclopedias. Both must grimace and mumble when my name shows up on their caller ID.

"What's he messed up this time? The furnace? The air conditioner? Maybe he has tried to fix the low-beam headlight by changing the high-beam bulb again."

The amazing thing about those boys is that, despite my never-ending needs, they answer their phones and talk to me. But, of all those responses, I am particularly grateful for the time Gene saved my life without the aid of wrenches or screwdrivers.

It was a winter of snow and confinement. I was five and Gene was four, and we were more than ready to play outside when permission was finally granted. The winds ceased, the sun came out, and our mom said it was okay to leave the trailer. She did not shove us out the door or tell us not to come back until spring. Instead she covered the be-careful rules and made sure that we were properly dressed.

To say we were bundled up was an understatement. We wore two pair of pants. Scarves and gloves and buttoned-up coats shielded the cold, and both of us strutted proudly in our dad's boots. We did not have our own; but, even if we had, we would have asked for his. I cannot remember the pair I used, but the top of Gene's black, rubber boots covered the legs of his pants.

The world looked new. The air was crisp and fresh, and everything was covered in white or ice glitter. In the over-sized footwear Gene and I waded through the snow and quickly forgot our promises. We went beyond the boundary lines that had been passionately established.

At the far end of the trailer park, possibly fifty yards from home, the non-stop snow and rain had created a temporary lake where mud puddles had formed in the summer. It was deeper in the middle but appeared to be frozen all over. The edge seemed solid enough, and the smooth ice was a slippery delight. We skated as gracefully as two boys ever did with boots on. Each successful glide brought a temptation to move farther away from the solid ground.

In the center a small log poked through and offered us a bench. I challenged Gene to race there but did not wait for him to be close enough for a fair start. I was twenty feet ahead when I reached the wooden seat and turned to celebrate the victory. In an instance the cheer turned to a choking gurgle as the ice broke, and I plunged into the frigid water.

With arms flailing I surfaced and struggled to hold on to whatever my hands hit. Chunks of ice continued to break, and I went under again and again. When I came up, Gene was shouting for help and giving advice. No one heard our screams, but his instructions still echo in my head.

"Flap your arms like a bird." He shouted it over and over and frantically demonstrated in case I had fluid in my ears.

I would guess that the water was a little deeper than I was tall. Because of the furious arm motion and the repeated jumps when my feet hit the bottom, my nose and head rose intermittently above the ice. I made grab after grab for something to hold on to. None too soon, I caught a section of ice that did not break. Gene extended his hand and helped pull my waterlogged body from the freezing water.

When we were almost to the bank, the ice beneath me cracked again. I lunged forward but did not go under. One of my dad's boots, however, was off my foot and wedged in the hole. We could see the top of it above the ice. Valiantly Gene bent over and tugged as hard as he could. Instead of retrieving it, he lost his balance and plunged part way in. His head and torso were submerged in the water. Only his kicking legs were visible. They moved like he was sprinting even though he was going nowhere.

Somehow I pulled him out, and somehow the boot was in his hand. I put it back on, and we limped home as best as we could.

As our mother pulled off our clothes, we all cried. Her tears were for two boys who had skated on thin ice. Gene and I cried because we thought something was biting us. We did not understand frostbite or the dangers of getting that cold. Innocently we thought that fish had swum into our shirts and pants when we went under.

After an eternity in hot water, our wrinkled bodies were allowed to get out of the tub. The sporadic fish bites had ceased, but our ears were just beginning to hurt. They were chewed on long into the night.

Edith, Forgive Us

Generally the house phone did not ring at five in the morning. If the roosters weren't crowing and a baby wasn't crying, it was leave-me-alone hour. This was especially true of Sunday mornings when we slept in until 8:00 a.m. After all, it was the day of rest.

"What's wrong?" Julie asked.

"Murray needs help. He wants my dad to come over, and they need me there. Go back to sleep."

The jeans and shirt and shoes were on the floor where I had thrown them the night before. A baseball cap covered my uncombed hair. It was cold enough for me to wear the heavy coat and gloves.

Once I negotiated the two miles of country curves and picked up Dad, it took only a few minutes to drive to Murray's. He had built a brick home that lay across the pasture from the two-story farm house that he had grown up in with his aunt, Clara Mary.

"Edith fell. She can't get up. That's all Murray said when he called. He's waiting on us," said my dad. It was too early for much more conversation than that when he got in the car.

We turned off the highway at Eggland. Mr. Carpenter no longer sold eggs, but the faded sign remained. Past the Engle farm and the Grammer household, we could see Murray in the driveway. The big man paced back and forth and wrenched his hands.

Murray wore flannel pajamas, light blue with cowboys and Indians on them. One pant leg was inside his boot and the other was on the outside. His hunting cap had the earflaps down. He must have been hiding his hair as well.

"Mr. Perkinson," he addressed my dad, "she can't get up. She went to the bathroom, and her knees gave out. She can't get up."

"Do we need to call an ambulance?"

"No, she just can't get up. Usually she can get up but not this morning. It's been an hour now. If you can get her back in bed, she'll be okay."

When I was a teenager, Murray hired me to work for him for two summers. In those days he assigned the chores as soon as I arrived, but this morning he was panicking. He needed help, and he wanted it now. Normally Murray could have lifted the corner of the house by himself, but stress had drained his strength.

Inside, his wife lay on the floor of their bedroom. She smiled and repeated what Murray had told us. Edith was a large woman. I did not believe that we could move her, but my father seemed ready for the challenge. After she sat up, his instructions flowed.

"You get on that side and reach under her arm and across her back. Reach under her knee with your other arm."

"Are you sure you can do this?" I questioned.

He nodded as we mirrored each other's motions and locked hands behind her back and under her knees. My dad was lanky and stout and in his sixties. Despite my doubts, we strained and lifted on the count of three. Edith was off the carpet, we had our balance, and the bed was only six feet away. Slowly but surely we moved backwards so that she could be placed on the edge of her bed. We held tightly, and Edith held on tightly to us.

"I got her!" Murray shouted when we were only a step away.

At that moment he dove on the bed with an earflap blocking his vision and extended his arms. He sat in the very spot that had been saved for Edith. Since he was in the way and since we could not stop, his wife was dropped on his lap. In a flash, she slid out of his arms, down his legs, and to the middle of the floor.

"I'm sorry. I just wanted to help," Murray apologized. "Edith, are you okay?"

She was fine, but we had failed.

"Murray, we are going to get this done, but we need you to watch and tell us when we're close enough to the bed. Tell us when it is safe to put her there."

"I sure will, Mr. Perkinson."

When everybody was ready, my dad and I picked a side and locked hands. On three we lifted and wobbled a little, but we were confident that we would get the job done.

"Murray, are we close enough?'

"Yes, Mr. Perkinson, you sure are!"

The excitement in his voice should have been a warning. In an instant he again jumped to the very place where we had hoped to set Edith. Since it was too late for him to move, his wife landed on his lap. In a flash, she slid out of his arms, down his legs, and to the middle of the floor.

We had sore backs and a growing uneasiness to work with Murray in the room. Yet we offered to try one more time. Unfortunately Murray attempted to catch her just as he had done before, and for the third time Edith flew to the center of the room.

I masked the frustration, but my heart was not kind. Secretly I wished that the Indians on his pajamas would remove the Elmer Fudd hat and scalp him. But, we were a Quaker community, and it was Sunday. The tribe needed some rest too.

Murray was more anxious than ever. He paced around her and could not stop clenching and unclenching his fists.

""It will be okay, Murray," Edith comforted in a calm tone. Her voice must have relaxed him enough for a moment of inspiration.

"Mr. Perkinson," he started as he straightened his hat, "I got a floor jack and a two by six out in the barn. Do you think we could slide the board under her and lift her with that?"

I reached for the phone before he finished the statement. The ambulance responded quickly to the 911 call. Within ten minutes Edith lay on a transport stretcher and was receiving medical attention.

My dad and I left before the x-rays could show how many times she had been dropped.

Jake

If not for the moonlight, darkness would have enveloped the outside world; but inside the apartment our modern conveniences provided all entertainment and illumination that we needed. That suddenly changed when the loss of power extinguished lamps and the television. A match flame allowed Julie to find a flashlight.

Randomly kerosene lanterns and wax candles lit up a few rooms in each house in the neighborhood. From our upstairs bedroom window, it was clear that no one had been spared. We could hear shouting in the park, and a burning smell tainted the air.

"Let's go outside to see what happened," I said.

In the center of Azalia was a section of land that the founders had set aside as the town square. Grass and trees provided a natural playground for the children. That evening, however, adults stood on the edge of the park and watched a dangerous display. They were mystified by a broken power line that snapped violently each time it touched the ground.

When the cable connected with the earth, massive sparks showered the area and smoke drifted upward from the soil. It hit once. Then twice. Then again and again. It was a reverse Fourth of July since the show was at ground level instead of in the sky.

"Jake, get out of there," cried one of the women

At the end of the park nearest the abandoned, interurban power station, a lantern swayed back and forth about three feet off the ground. The smoke and darkness made it hard to see the man who held it.

"Jake, it's not safe," yelled someone.

"Keep away from it," called another.

In response to the warnings, the old man waved the light and bellowed out good advice.

"Stand back. Don't come any closer," he commanded as he approached the broken line.

We will never know whether he reacted to a specific voice or to a nudge from God, but sighs of relief were breathed when he retreated towards his house. Jake was like that. Despite his slow movement, the old man would appear unexpectedly and disappeared just as quickly. Like the broken, whipping cable, he did not stay long in any one spot.

The Jake I knew may not have represented the potential that had been shared with family and community in years past. He seemed disconnected from normal activities. He was always alone and could often be spotted wandering through cemeteries where he collected the plastic flowers that filled his car.

A few summers earlier, jogging had been on my exercise list. I ran daily and had started complaining less and less. Every once in a while I even added some distance to push the limits. One evening my feet weren't pounding into the asphalt like they usually did. In fact, they barely seemed to touch the surface, and I felt at ease with the pace and the extra miles.

On the way back and still a mile from home I jumped off the road and into a ditch when tires screeched and a vehicle slid sideways past me. When it stopped, Jake opened the door and stepped out with a puzzled look on his face.

"Whose boy are you?" he asked in a loud, monotone voice.

His volume and the car that blocked my path demanded an answer. Limbs that had been so light suddenly were heavy and tired. Sweat blinded me as I gasped for air.

With hands resting on my knees I responded, "I'm Lester Perkinson's son." At twenty-two, I refused to call myself a boy.

Seemingly unimpressed, Jake nodded and muttered, "Huh." After that he started his car and drove off.

My legs felt stiff and sore as I inched out of the ditch and walked back home. Jake probably reached Azalia in five minutes, but I was late for supper. As was his nature, he had appeared unexpectedly and disappeared too quickly for me to ask for a ride.

Rally Round the Ranger

Sons of Anarchy or Hell's Angels? It was hard to identify the phrases that had been sewn on the backs of the bikers who passed on each side of my truck. Even if I hadn't been worried, I would have wondered what was printed on the jackets and vests in front of me and behind me.

The roar of Harleys vibrated through the floorboard of my truck and muted the radio music. I tried not to look in the rear view mirror, but ignoring their presence was not an easy option.

Something besides the shaking of my vehicle did not feel right. Four in front, ten behind, and a stop light that would not turn green. The afternoon had been pleasant, and I prayed that I had been good enough. Yet the revelry and the revving engines seemed specifically for my benefit. The mind plays funny games, but there was little humor when two more motorcycles flanked the passenger side of my Ford Ranger. Then, to complete the escort, a rider pulled up beside me and knocked on the window.

With what semblance of courage I could muster, I put on a happy face and prayed as I gazed into a heavy beard and dark sunglasses. Thick, long hair fell from a helmet that crowned a solid man. There was little doubt that the worn, leather jacket confirmed his road-warrior status. Hopefully my voice wouldn't crack when I responded.

I rolled down the window, but before anything could be said, he leaned in, grinned, and shouted, "Coach, how are you? It's me. David!"

21

For the second time in my life, I was glad to meet David Hudson. The conversation was far too short, but it was pleasant. Even though David had intentionally put me on edge, I was glad he took time to say hello.

As he and his thundering herd pulled away waving and laughing, I thought about the first time he walked into the wrestling room. He wore an AC/DC t-shirt with the sleeves ripped off. That was not uncommon in the gym, but it made the move-in stand out from his peers. From the looks of the biceps, he could wear whatever he wanted.

After two days of workouts one of the varsity wrestlers tapped me on the shoulder and pointed at the newcomer. "Do you think he'll stay?"

A part-time optimist and a coach without a heavyweight, I quietly said "We'll see," but my eyes pleaded for a sign from the war god that our big-man prayers had been answered. At the end of practice my begging was rewarded when David came back to the room.

"Coach, what can I do better? I want that spot. I want to be on this team."

The question was sincere and his eagerness was far more boyish than his frame. I hesitated for a moment because a well-positioned pause can make a person appear to be wise. But, in truth, the answer he needed was the very one that might drive him away.

"You've got some time to make a decision, but you'll never be eligible to compete until you get a trim. It's a wrestling rule."

With hair hanging below his shoulders David had that ancient, warrior look. Yet, despite the menacing aura, he was a lovable giant when no score was being kept. That evening he shed his Attila-the-Hun locks. They had been sheared, but the high-and-tight, military haircut still exuded a powerful stay-out-of-my-space message. With or without the long hair David was all about attitude and presence.

Two weeks later he hesitated and then approached slowly after the rest of the team headed off for stair laps.

"I just can't do it anymore. I have to quit."

Almost too crushed to speak, I searched for words but only needed a syllable.

"Why?"

"I can't run on the concrete. I cut off the toes of my foot with a lawn mower two summers ago. The accident kept me out of school most of last year. That's why I didn't wrestle then."

As he described the unfortunate incident, David dropped to the mat and removed a shoe and then a sock. He felt a need to prove the problem. Being a part of a team must have been awfully important to him if he was willing to endure that much pain every day.

Compromise is easy when both parties want the same thing. Riding a stationary bike and jumping rope on the mat would replace the stairs and sprints. In return, the team picked up a fierce competitor. David did not win every match but he was tough. What a dichotomy: a beast on the mat who loved cartoons, companions, and the Three Stooges after Saturday practices.

The next time I run into David, I hope he still values fellowship and has a great sense of humor. But, my heart might not take it if the motorcycles surround me again.

Confusion

When Mom got out of the car, I moved up to the seat beside my dad. My arm hung out the window while I watched the building and tried to ignore my brothers and sisters. The inside of the car had become a playground. The smaller siblings hopped from the front to the back and then from the back to the front. No one was safe from shoes or elbows, and at first no one minded.

We had driven to Jeffersonville so my mother could spend time with a relative who lived at the care center. Mom was beautiful and vibrant, but the ladies inside were old and feeble. Most sat motionless on the chairs and couches. Others seemed to bend to the floor as they pushed their walkers.

The over-the-seat competition was wearing on my nerves. I probably should not have shoved my brother when his knee caught my chin. Just when I thought my dad was going to give me the discipline look, a resident pointed in our direction through the open window in her room.

She waved someone over and explained, "Come here. You have to see him. It's my boy. The one out front." She repeated it over and over again.

"Aren't you coming in?" she called to me.

The question was simple enough, and her voice was endearing. But, the confusion was intense. Her boy would not have been eight, but she longed to see the eight-year-old she had once known. I did not understand her condition and could not comprehend why she might be at a care center instead of with her son.

24

As a third grader, I did not know that a mom and child could be separated. I did not know that a mom could forget her child. Yet, even then, I wondered if I might someday be just as uncertain about who was really standing in front of me.

Years later, when I was in my forties, two ladies reawakened that memory and some of the questions that accompanied it. My dad and I were helping a neighbor change rooms in a similar facility. We moved some items from the old room to the new one and brought some of her personal belongings from the car. Carts and families and residents were sidestepped. We accidentally bumped into a few visitors who carried as many boxes as we did.

Suddenly an energetic elder, a Granny Clampett look-alike, jumped in front of me. The woman hardly weighed anything and stood only shoulder high to me. She was a curiosity, especially with the fifteen belts across her forearm.

"My roommate thinks I steal?"

"I doubt that. What in the world would you steal?"

"Belts! She says I take belts. Why would anyone take somebody's belt?"

My hesitant "I don't know" and puzzled look finished the conversation. I headed back towards the room that I was supposed to be working in, and she searched frantically for the next person that she could tell about the allegations that had been made against her.

I was almost to my dad when it happened again. Another resident, also a very small lady, caught my attention. She sat alone in the privacy of her room and stared into the hallway.

25

When I said "Hello," she lifted her left hand and motioned for me to enter. As I stepped to the doorway, she stopped rocking the wooden chair and leaned forward. Her grin widened and her eyes sparkled. Something amused her.

Then she caught me off guard. The tiny, frail figure giggled, raised her hand, and offered an unfriendly gesture, and a whispered, "You're a _____!"

Use your imagination for the descriptor, but know this: Everyone in the building was not as confused as I was that day. She was pretty perceptive. A lot of folks would assure you that she pegged me accurately.

Nudge Me Gently

Towards Faith in Youth

Daughter Hannah

"Children are the world's most valuable resource and its best hope for the future."

John F. Kennedy

Home Grown

It was a routine business practice. When Bud Jines opened the fruit stand each summer, the "home grown" signs were posted near the tomatoes and whatever else was for sale. Even if the vegetables came from another county or state, the declaration was still displayed.

Bud justified it by saying, "They're grown at somebody's home."

At twelve I could make two dollars a day selling produce at the market or twenty five cents an hour in the watermelon fields. In the mornings I was parking my bike when the chugging of the John Deere announced Bud's approach. He crested the hill standing behind the wheel like the skipper of a green ship. He never sat down and never explained why. He wore a sleeveless, white t-shirt, the kind with the thin straps. Sunlight often glimmered off the gold chain that hooked his wallet to his belt.

Sorting through the woven, shaved-wood baskets was the first duty of the day. If a tomato went bad, I wheeled and rifled it towards the trees. The one directly behind the market split about thirty feet up. The limbs forked like a slingshot and offered a challenge.

If there was a little league game that evening, I got some early practice by throwing the rotten tomatoes through the opening. I only missed once. Unfortunately that happened when State Trooper Dallas Norman had parked his freshly waxed car under the tree.

The pay for working at the fruit stand and in the watermelon fields was not going to make any of us rich, but ten to twelve bucks a week let me open a savings account. And, there was a tasty, fringe benefit. When a melon was accidentally dropped, we could eat all we could grab.

In the years that followed, Gene and I picked up seasonal work on a lot of farms. Prior to Thanksgiving we caught turkeys. We bailed hay and straw, picked sweet corn, and even milked goats for a week. Stalls needed to be cleaned, and fences were built. We once unloaded a semi of chunk coal by hand.

One summer Gene received an offer that was not based on hourly wages when our neighbor suggested a partnership. Mr. Catlin would provide the land and materials. Gene and Kenny Baldwin would supply the labor. And, when the harvest was over, fifty percent of the sales went to Mr. Catlin and the other fifty to Gene and Kenny. They hoped to make it big in the gherkin market.

The field was prepared, and the seed was planted. After his other work was finished that summer, Gene headed to the cucumber patch. Except for Kenny, nobody hoed any harder or kept a sharper eye on a crop. Picking the cucumbers when they were thumb size was the key to a fortune.

Now they may have miscalculated the potential for profit. After hours of crawling through the two acres on their hands and knees, they loaded the truck and hauled their first harvest to Brown County. Gene's share was six dollars. The next few trips were pretty much the same. If money was to be made, they would need a bigger load of the smaller cucumbers.

However, just as the make-it-or-break-it crop was almost ready, it rained and rained and rained. It may not have been for forty days and forty nights, but it seemed like it. When the deluge receded, the pickin's looked as big as canoes. There was not a tiny one in sight. Despite the monstrous size, they gleaned the field and took a truck load of colossal, green cucumbers to market. Unfortunately, it was not a profit maker.

When I visit our daughter April's grave, I have been known to tell her about the infamous cucumber patch that had been planted a hundred yards below her. I explain how envious of Uncle Gene I was; and she hears that even though he made almost nothing, I never heard a complaint. Gene made an honest effort and trusted Mr. Catlin. The only promises were that the work would be hard and that it was an opportunity. He accepted both as a part of the business venture.

What we become in life is influenced by how we are raised and how we face the rainy days and storms as best we can. Many of us ease into a day just like we are working at that fruit stand. We look for the good, throw out the bad, and market the best we have. A big part of who we become is home grown, but a portion of our character may have been influenced by our neighbors.

Heroes

My afternoon bus duty allowed me to say goodbye to a lot of students and hello to the driver who parked where I was stationed. I enjoyed teaching English, but standing outside was usually a comfortable way to end the day.

"Are you doing okay?" was the typical greeting to the bus driver. Each afternoon a mass of energy swarmed out of the school at dismissal time, and some of it headed his way.

"Sure am," was always his reply. He spoke quietly.

I particularly liked the kids who boarded his vehicle, but I kept an eye on the whole crew. At least one of them was a Ninja warrior with a pea shooter. When I least expected it, a clandestine assault sent a projectile flying at my bald head. The sneaky lad was an expert shot who could mask the joy of a direct hit until the bus pulled away.

It was early spring and still a little cold, so I zipped up my jacket. When I looked in on the driver that afternoon, it was evident that something was wrong. He had slumped forward on the steering wheel, and his skin was extremely pale.

I jumped up the steps and asked, "Are you okay?"

He tried to respond, but his words were garbled.

"The bus driver's really sick," I said. The tone expressed an emergency and a call to attention. As I leaned him back and checked his breathing, three unsolicited responses proved invaluable.

"I know where the principal is," said the young man who raced out the door for help.

The next to exit shouted, "The nurse will be right here."

"I'll have the office call 911," promised the last one.

The other passengers sat quietly waiting to hear what they could do. The quick-thinking trio had covered the immediate needs. They had taken no time to discuss options. Each accepted a role and raced for assistance. Shortly afterwards the school personnel arrived, and moments later the ambulance pulled in to assist the stroke victim. Thankfully, the driver made it.

Those young men were resourceful. They acted immediately and helped a man who always took care of them. None were schoolboy celebrities or athletes or honor roll students, but they were unbelievably aware of everything around them. To be honest, all three were among my pea-shooter suspects. Keeping track of where everyone stood probably allowed that individual to go undetected when aim was taken at the top of my head. But, on that day, the same skill delivered medical attention to the bus driver.

I grew up with entertainment heroes, crusaders who saved the day on a regular basis. Some arrived on Saturday mornings, but others showed up throughout the month to make the world a safer place. My favorites were on TV and at bookstands and often postured in iconic outfits that included masks and capes and insignias.

For me, it has always been a bothersome notion that most were strangers. Superman came from distant planet.   The Lone Ranger roamed the West, not his hometown.   In *Highway to Heaven* an angel walked into neighborhoods to provide a touch of grace.   Why is it that so many people wait for strangers to save the day?

Like others I have had the privilege to meet, those three students stepped forward and did what they could.   No weekly series depicts their exploits.   No admirers say to their buddies, "Hey, let's pretend we're thirteen and save the bus driver."   But, there are still heroes among us like the boys who rode on the bus that day. Hopefully, some live close by.

Compassion

The cemetery dominated the landscape as our plane approached Washington, DC. Arlington was the first recognizable site from above. It would be the last visible piece of history when we departed to Indianapolis. I had a conference to attend, but I also wanted to visit monuments and museums. There were significant stories to be absorbed.

The symposium proved to be tourist friendly since portions of each day were unscheduled. Even at that, my to-do list had to be trimmed. The Viet Nam War Memorial and a first visit to the Holocaust Museum would not be eliminated. Neither would Arlington National Cemetery.

At the Lincoln Memorial, an official felt it necessary to remind the guests that they were at a place of honor. Reverence was deserved. Courtesy was expected. I do not know what had happened before I arrived, but I sensed that no one felt the guidance was undeserved or that the infraction had been intentional. It was my last stop before catching the subway to the cemetery.

Being seated for a while was a relief since wearing new shoes on the trip had proven to be a bad idea. My feet blistered before I realized that there was a problem. Band aids and doubling up with two pairs of thin socks eased the discomfort, but my pace had slowed down considerably. It helped that Arlington was extremely crowded. Hurrying was not going to be an option.

On vacations, Julie tries to convince me that I do not have to do everything there is to do just because we are there. Initially that was an unacceptable notion. If I paid the money for the trip, how dare I not be a part of everything there was to do? No wonder vacations wore me out. Before I left home this time, I promised her that I would limit the rushing and enjoy the experiences that I found time for.

The ceremonial changing of the guards at the Tomb of the Unknown Soldier and the endless rows of Americans who had made great sacrifices for their country was touching. The heat from the flame at the Kennedy grave site surprised me. The names on some of the headstones were familiar, but I wished for a better grasp of heroes.

Two hours later, I limped back towards the subway station. Ahead of me was a group of high school students. There might have been eight. They had come face to face with history and were excited to tell each other what they had seen. They walked almost as slowly as I did as they shared what they had learned.

One spoke up, and everyone else politely waited for a turn. They were teaching. Some wished they had taken a different path. The classmates were not sure how they had missed or overlooked what a friend had seen. I doubt anyone had time to take a breath until one of the girls wheeled and addressed the young man who lagged behind.

"You are never this quiet. Come on. Who did you see?"

His reply took a moment. He cleared his throat before he answered.

"I have been with my grandfather. He is buried here."

Most visitors came that day to take in what they could about our nation's past. People stooped to read the markers. Some took picture. Many had questions. But, like a few others who paused at a specific graveside that afternoon, the young man had a personal agenda. He came to connect with family.

You could have heard a pin drop when he hesitated and said, "I have been with my grandfather."

The young lady deserved a hug when she responded, "Tell us about him."

The friends immediately stopped and listened, and I stepped around them.

A Better Generation

Every once in a while Mr. Erne informed the student body that he expected a little more. I appreciated a principal who asked us to be responsible citizens and trusted that he could confide in us. And, what faith he must have had if he believed that we were attentive to the entire intercom message.

In those days Columbus High School consisted of sophomores, juniors, and seniors. It was a time when loudspeaker announcements provided daily timeouts. A substitute teacher who chose storytelling over lesson plans was just as welcome, but other distractions were readily available to the mind or eye. Hairstyles and the human anatomy interrupted my concentration more than the principal ever did.

It seems to me that values must have eroded greatly during the time that I sat in those classes. When I was a sophomore, Mr. Erne pointed out that one percent of the population caused most of the problems that he was concerned with. However, by the senior year, he raised that to five percent. Apparently the class of '71 had not been good listeners or leaders.

That same moral decline followed me to college. When I was junior, the street-corner preacher stood right outside my dorm. He prayed for an end of violence and regularly implied that the Indiana State Sycamores were the descendants of the Sodom and Gomorrah communities and the cause of all calamities. He warned of a fire and brimstone purification and prophesied the arrival of the Apocalypse. His lunch-hour ministry did not draw a crowd, but having no audience to speak to did not temper the threats. An intercom system would have put less strain on his voice.

My sins are certainly listed on the Big Guy's scroll, but I doubt that I am solely responsible for the four percent increase that Mr. Erne made note of. Sometimes I embellished my exploits, but admitting that I did not read a Shakespeare assignment will not bring any fist-shaking congratulations from Folsom Prison. Even picking a few flowers from a university garden has probably been forgiven by now, especially since I had just finished *Daffodils* by William Wordsworth before they were plucked from the earth.

However, my attempt at humor nearly started a riot on a return flight from Florida. I appreciated the refreshments that were served but had tired of the lack of creativity. It would have been a tremendous change of pace if the airline snacks had occasionally included a milkshake or a piece of pecan pie. Would you not be in love with the lady who announced, "My mom just picked twenty quarts of strawberries so we're all having homemade sundaes after you fasten your seat belts"?

Well, I am sorry to say that I don't believe that will ever happen. Maybe that is why I nodded at the stewardess and cupped my hand over the package when she handed me the peanuts. As she was about to pass, I said, "Thank you so much for the cashews!"

"Cashews? Can I have cashews?" blurted a gullible soul who was seated in the front.

"Is there a chance you have any sunflower seeds?" begged another.

The flight was not delayed, but the requests continued as she moved down the aisle.

Even the passengers who could clearly see that I only had peanuts were asking about options. I may have been the catalyst for fifty percent of the problems on that trip.

My girls are no more accepting of my willingness to provoke a laugh than that pilot was. Their Grandmother Perkinson has read the Bible frontwards and backwards multiple times. Their Grandfather Darling is a minister, and Mom Julie is obviously a preacher's kid. For the most part, these young ladies were raised in an ethical environment that Mr. Erne would have been pleased with.

To the best of my memories, the first time I witnessed their unwavering sense of right and wrong happened when Julie and I allowed our elementary-aged daughters to walk to my parents' home. It was a two mile trek across country roads, and they were proud to embark. The distance was covered in record time.

Perception is an unjust judge at times. When they walked into her house, Grandma Perkinson had asked where Julie and I were. When the girls announced that they had walked all the way by themselves, Grandma said something like, "You did not."

Our phone rang immediately. "Come and get us. Grandma called us liars."

To this day, I don't believe that is what my mother intended to convey. It was meant to be a statement of surprise not a denial of their trip. Obviously my girls took telling the truth to a higher level than their dad did.

The last time we discussed honesty with a daughter was when Hannah was sixteen and looking for her first job. She would interview, come out satisfied that she was loved and might already have a raise, and then get a call the next day that she was not a good fit for the position.

Finally I asked, "Can you tell me about the interview?"

"They just ask me questions. They laugh when I say something funny. And, they talk about what the job would involve."

"Anything else?"

"There's a survey that has some odd questions," she reflected.

I explored a little with, "Tell me about it too."

She immediately clarified what bothered her the most. "Well, they asked if I liked people, and I marked *NO*."

"Hannah, they weren't asking if you preferred being alone or if you wanted to go to anybody's family reunion. They just wanted to know if you would be helpful and nice to the customers."

It was then that I realized that she too had inherited the let's-be-overly-honest trait from her mother. Her next comment confirmed the deduction.

"I don't care what you think it meant," she asserted. "I'm not going to hell for a survey question."

There is a strong chance that this generation is back on track.

Step to the Music

Mrs. Hoppock and Mrs. Tolle helped the children at the Sandcreek-Azalia Friends Vacation Bible School. Thankfully, all the ladies who worked with us were fairly tolerant. Budding artists and the leaders of tomorrow needed some space to make their own unique contributions.

At six my friends and I were dependent on the teachers for Kool-Aid and cookies and supplies, but at the project tables we were not held accountable to the same conformity that accompanied Bible lessons and Sunday school songs. Obviously our Popsicle-stick creations looked similar each year, but no one measured angles or graded our efforts. At the end of the day, Mrs. Hoppock smiled. At the end of the week, Mrs. Tolle let us take the crafts home.

One morning Elmer the Bull stared at me while I created a masterpiece. I would like to think that he approved, but it was hard to tell. He did not smile as much as his wife Elsie the Cow did on the dairy products that carried her logo, but why would he? Her face adorned the cartons and packages of creamy, mouth-watering products that were kept in the refrigerated displays. His was pasted on a tube that should never be put in anyone's mouth.

A bead of white bubbled from the tip of the Elmer's Glue bottle in front of me. Pretty soon it rolled slowly down the plastic spout towards the table top. To keep everything clean, wasted globs of thick adhesive had been smeared on the remnants of colored paper that littered the table. What got on my hand was rubbed fiercely into the legs of my blue jeans.

Not quite satisfied, I added two more jewels to the paper in front of me. After putting too much glue on the back the plastic trinkets, I pressed the invaluable emeralds and rubies on the construction-paper crown until I felt my worth was justified. None of the princes or princesses around me saw a need for the same design. One or two had an artisan's vision and a steady hand for neat lines and scissor work. A fewS hurried to be done first.

When the glue dried, we placed the caps on our heads. Our egos soared as adjustments were made and the backs were taped for an appropriate fit. And once the finished crowns confirmed our royalty, we were rewarded immediately when a box of toy instruments was carried in and placed on the floor. We would play for our own coronation.

There were rules for learning the church songs. "Start when Mrs. Fisher nods. Stand straight. Sing a little louder. Remember the words." And, eventually we would know that there was plenty of forgiveness and laughter for those who were fidgety and forgetful when the these-kids-don't-sing-together-much-except-at-vacation-bible-school choir delivered its best on Sunday morning.

Everyone made a mad dash for the horns and drums. Some lost their royal hats in the process. Tambourines, cymbals, and tapping sticks were available for those who were fast enough. What I would have given for a cowbell! Except for, "Be careful" and "Don't hurt anyone," there were no commandments that had to be memorized before we could play in the band.

After each of my friends had picked a musical device, a little separation was required.

Instinctively we lined up with some distance between each other so that a flutist's inspired dance might not lead to an instrument in someone's eye and so that none of us got slugged by a percussionist. Basically Quakers are a non-violent lot, but our drums and triangles were meant to be pounded just like anyone else's. Clobbering them while not inadvertently assaulting a neighbor demanded a great deal of focus and some space between us.

Unlike Joshua at the battle of Jericho our band did not circle the area seven times, but we marched and blew and clanged until we were dizzy. The line weaved in and out of the annex. We went round the room and through the kitchen and past the scary door whose veneered grain sketched the foreboding shape of Satan himself. And every few minutes the next person in line stepped to the front and led us. It made me nervous when Andy guided us past the crafts, through the door with the ominous image, and then directly into the meetinghouse.

Since lightning did not strike and the adults did not scold, the music and stomping of feet grew louder and louder as we passed by the pulpit. Each new leader kept us inside the sanctuary and looked for an original path around and through the pews. We may not have made a beautiful sound, but every boy and girl made a joyful noise. For the most part, our heartbeats provided the only true rhythm that day as we embraced the moment and the chance to be leaders.

Thoreau once said, "If a man loses pace with his companions, perhaps it is because he hears a different drummer. Let him step to the music which he hears, however measured, or far away." I don't remember him, but Henry David must have attended Vacation Bible School too.

Motion and Magic and Playgrounds

"Just one more time!" echoed through the park. Though the voices changed, the cry was constant. One child and then another made a case for staying longer. A few adults checked their watches and sighed deeply. Some responded with "Five more minutes" as if saying a number would make the adrenaline evaporate into the clouds.

Like the rest, my three raced across the playground and lunged at unoccupied equipment and leaped off everything. One after another the traditionalists slid down the slides while the more defiant whelps straddled the outer edges and climbed up. Collisions happened, but casualties did not.

There were few introductions and little advantage in identifying so many first-time acquaintances. Their spirits knew each other. All the children were related by motion. Brothers and sisters and kinetic cousins played tag and took turns spinning the merry-go-round until it was time to jump on with the rest.

Energy was the ticket to an hour of adventure. Technique did not necessarily provide a higher status, but it could be learned. Gifted acrobats glided one hand after another across the monkey bars as admirers awaited a turn. Novices pushed their parents away when they had seen enough to mimic the more graceful gymnasts.

Apprentice magicians waved their hands and invited grownups to enjoy the enchantment of the swings. Spells were cast that subtracted the years that numbered more than fingers.

Somehow parents gradually became as youthful as the children who accompanied them. It was as if the repetitive swaying equalized their ages. Favorite aunts, teens, moms and dads.... No one was immune. The gentle movement provided an opportunity to relax and rejuvenate.

At the swing sets time did not matter. Smiles widened, and eyes sparkled. Where one person stood behind and shoved the other, quiet chuckles and pleasant conversation were exchanged. Roles switched when pushers became swingers and swingers pushed. And, unlike the solo daredevils who self-propelled themselves to the sky, the swing partners were content to be nudged forward again and again.

Unfortunately the experience had to end. Expressing their feelings in silence, couples strolled off hand in hand. Youngsters, uneasy with too much peace, broke away for one last, wild slide. But, the most ardent performers did not leave the swings without executing a signature move.

In each group the boldest jumped on a swing seat and absorbed the instructions. "Sit still and hang on tight" was the ungrammatical gist of it. The decree was followed by an endless twisting. The chains that held the seat that held the body that held the beloved soul were wound and wound until they could not be turned one more time. Then suddenly the linked ropes were released, and a blurry circle was drawn in the air. As the uncoiling accelerated, a flurry of screams and shrieks erupted.

When the rapid swirling ceased, the hands that had squeezed the links so obediently did not release their grip until both feet were planted. The finale started with a spectacular, unrehearsed, dizzying dance. Arms grabbed for support that jelly legs could not provide. Knees buckled, and eyes bobbed as they searched for focus. The climax was a customary collapse and a series of wobble giggles. A slurred voice might laughingly beg, "Just one more time" from the grass.

At the playground my daughters practiced for the blistering pace of the years that lay ahead of them. They pushed both the swings and the limits. They faced challenges and met new faces and, most importantly, invited me to be with them as best I could. And, if I got a little woozy from watching a million somersaults and a thousand pirouettes, the little girls let me sit on the park bench in the shade. They learned to take care of me too.

Nudge Me Gently

Towards Responsibility

Wedding Day

"C'mon people now,
Smile on your brother
Ev'rybody get together
Try and love one another right now"

- The Youngbloods, *Get Together*

Never Easy, Rarely Free

Sometimes I have persistent cravings for cereal and Cracker Jacks. Snack food has obviously been a weakness, but it is the prize inside the box that drives the compulsion. Getting something for nothing always sounds like a good thing.

Once children learn to read, it is hard to hold them back unless they fixate on a single word. My shopping skills, for example, leveled out all too soon when I understood the meaning of F-R-E-E. After that, the taste of the flakes made no difference once I spotted the word *free* on the box, and I was not the only one. Many a skirmish has occurred in the cereal aisle as moms picked one brand while the cart-riding readers demanded the box with the gift inside.

Cracker Jacks came in the container with the blue-suited sailor boy on it. Sweet, sticky popcorn and a few hidden nuts would never have been so appealing without the inexpensive treasure that was hidden inside. Not many treats offered something to get stuck in our teeth and something to unwrap at the same time.

Each box was different, wasn't it? Sometimes syrupy kernels were all you could see when the package was opened; sometimes the miniature incentive was right on top. I cannot remember a specific surprise, but I knew that whatever I found was mine to do with as I wished and to shove in my brother's face if he chose a candy bar instead. Obviously, Snickers got its name because everyone laughed at the fools who did not get anything free with the nuts.

Somewhere along the line there is the danger of believing in getting something at no cost, and it isn't just about the money. It's also about wanting to be free from long-term obligations. Take the Cracker Jack prize. It was mine. I could give it away, keep it for a while, lose it, or toss it in the trash can. The choices were not very important. There was an eagerness to open the wrapper but almost none to keep the item.

We all make choices on a regular basis. In Sunday school class I never recited all the books of the Bible. It was easier to memorize New Testament and Old Testament and to use the index for the rest. For me, those two sections could be condensed into simple lessons, the promise of land and the promise of a child. First came the "land of milk and honey." It was followed by "unto you a child is born." Still stuck on *free*, I felt a little disappointed. No matter how hard I looked through the Good Book, I could never find the promise that there would be servants and nannies to do my work.

Can you imagine listening to those weary people in the desert when they discussed the land of milk and honey?

"The lambs will need a lot of water. Are we getting an irrigation system in Canaan or at least an outdoor pump at every house?"

"What do you think the market price is? Before we move, we ought to trade this old sandlot in for some mules. Better yet, you never know how important a little donkey might be."

But I suppose the pessimist in the group always added, "Wait a minute. Who's going to do all this work? I've gotten used to sunning myself out here in the desert on a regular basis.

Living somewhere else is starting to sound a lot like a job. I'm willing to hold an umbrella over someone, but that's it."

Now I understand that guy. Sunshine was free. He had grown accustomed to the harsh conditions even though he complained about them on a regular basis. He and I would have picked a similar cereal since we are both a little misguided. If opportunity knocked, we'd go deaf.

The "milk and honey" concept is tremendously labor intensive. Somebody had to herd the cattle and to protect the grazing land. A few of the lucky ones might even be chosen to stick their hands all the way into the beehive for the sweet stuff. Eventually there would be other occupations like a butcher, a baker, and a candlestick maker, but let's focus on the shepherding and farming for a moment.

Once you owned the estate, you inherited physical assignments. Sweat and calluses came with the territory. It was a home that had to be maintained, not a vacation resort with the pampering, five-star service. Deadlines, goals, and commitment came with the property.

Someone in the Bible was always announcing that a child was on the way. There was definitely no rest for the wicked or for those who had kids. Changing diapers and feeding the masses while they endured the plagues and battled Assyrians were arduous assignments. Teaching the boys to use slings and to trade with the Egyptians took time. With all that to do the daily chores must have been overwhelming. There were never enough hours in the day for milking the goats, polishing the camel saddle, and studying the Book of Begats.

And, no one was off the hook. Joseph and Mary had their hands full with that little child of Bethlehem. After all, raising a leader is a monumental task. Teaching someone to be prepared for the future puts a lot of pressure on everyone involved. When I hear "It takes a village to raise a child," I hope I have done my part. If not, I am sure that someone has been placed on this earth to remind me of it.

To tell you the truth, those nomads must have been as worn out as we are. Any of us would like to start the day by opening a box of cereal and getting the freebies, but at the end of the day, we have to earn our keep. We all know that having a place to live and children around us are wonderful promises, but taking care of them involves hard work and responsible decisions.

For a Tuppence

This summer my bird feeder has been filled every day. The seed is for songbirds, but all God creatures must have heard about it and the nearby water pond. A frisky squirrel and a chipmunk are regulars. The mourning doves are not shy about joining the cardinals and wrens and robins. Even a rabbit has stopped by.

Unlike the flowers in the butterfly garden, I cannot identify every bird, but that has not kept me from enjoying their company. The small ones arrive early. They sit on the feeder and sort through the mixture. They eat what they like and toss the rest to the ground. Grain flies everywhere when the sparrows sit on the wooden pegs and dig for their favorites. As the feeder empties, the after-lunch crew flies in and cleans the lawn. By the end of the day nothing has been wasted.

My intentions must have been suspect at first. If I went out the front door and sat on the porch, the wildlife scattered in every direction. Offering sustenance and water did not build an immediate trust, but that changed after a month.

One morning the smallest birds did not fly off, and the squirrel did not climb away when I relaxed on the bench and read the newspaper. It felt good to be accepted. They continued to eat while I deadheaded flowers before breakfast. As I swept the front steps and picked up a little, my mind wandered back a few weeks.

When I left my office at the end of the school year, I passed a young lady who carried a heavy basket of clothes. She would take ten steps, stop to get a better grip, and then place her knee under the whole load. She strained to kick the plastic hamper above her waist so that her arms could encircle it. All that shifting did not appear to make a difference. It was more than she needed to be hauling.

I turned the car around, introduced myself, and offered her a ride. The relief on her face was instant. She nodded and nervously put the basket in the back seat. When I asked where she wanted to go, she gave directions, but her voice was barely audible. I deciphered the instructions and headed there. She said it was not far. We drove two miles. I wondered how many times she had lugged that weight across town.

She might have been sixteen. She might have been twenty. Regardless, I felt like I was feeding the birds again. She needed the help but might have been concerned for her safety. Once she wiped a tear as I tried to talk with her. Maybe she was just that tired. Maybe she was rethinking her decision to get in the car even though I never meant to frighten her. When we arrived, she smiled and thanked me softly. On the way home, I hoped I had done the right thing. I wondered if I could have done it better.

In the *Feed the Birds* scene *in Mary Poppins*, pigeons surrounded an old woman at the steps of a cathedral where she sold breadcrumbs for a tuppence. They were fed for little or nothing. Appropriately the reverence of the tune emphasized the importance of doing the little things to help others. But, how long did it take for the birds to trust that the square was truly a sanctuary for them?

For a lifetime, I have watched my family and friends extend a hand to those about them.

They have fed the birds, provided for the hungry, and given what they could when there was a need. It doesn't hurt to remember that offering assistance and building trust go hand in hand. The gift is important but even more so if it is accepted.

Emptiness and Pain

The corned beef and cabbage with carrots and potatoes was why I chose the Irish restaurant, but I never dreamed how much food would come on the plate. At my request the waiter returned with a carry-out container and some plasticware before the first bite had been taken.

There was plenty of time to savor the meal and to strategize. I was ready to eat, but the man whom I had passed on the sidewalk might have been starving. He was hungry and homeless and a block away, and I was not quite sure how to offer him a meal. Yet, when the crème brulee was finished, I had a thought.

Instead of reaching for coins or glancing away as I approached him, I asked, "Could you help me? Is there a place around here to drop off some food? My room doesn't have a fridge or a microwave."

We became partners when he responded, "I'll take care of it for you."

Leaving one meal didn't change the big picture, but maybe it helped the moment. Too often the face of hunger sits close by, doesn't it? Its haggard features nest on street corners. Its eyes stare blankly from the pictures in magazines. Whatever the origin, the piercing glares guilt me into asking, "Is this the one I should help?"

Obviously most of us have seen hunger. I suppose I have even felt it, but I have not lived it. Eating late is an inconvenience. Missing breakfast is a choice. A belly growl is an insignificant faux pas that does not increase empathy or an understanding of the cruel condition.

In a world of seeming plenty there are problems that are hard to fathom. And if we can't quite comprehend physical hunger, then how difficult is it to grasp that there are those who so full of something and yet so completely empty at the same time? It's what I call the sated void.

Were you ever consumed by a worry that was big enough to become the first thing you thought of in the morning and the last thing on your mind and heart when you fell asleep at night? And then it occupied your every waking thought as the concern announced itself a thousand times. An overwhelming trouble like that stuffs itself into the void it creates and expands until the pain is almost unbearable.

None of us face exactly the same challenges in life, and some paths are rockier than others. The journey to emptiness is unique enough for the individuals who face it, but the basic problems can be identified. Grief and anger and regret can fill a body until there is no room for love of self or anyone else. So can shame and fear and depression. And they have partners like hunger who join them in gnawing at hope until the spirit, like the body, is indigent and starving.

Did you know that a cake that is starting to get a little dry can be revived with bread? Now admittedly cake doesn't last very long at my house, but on the rare occasions when only a few pieces are eaten, the exposed surface can be protected by placing a piece or two against it. The moisture transfers from the bread to the cake and keeps it fresh.

Wouldn't it be great if it were that easy to help people, if we could just carry around a daily slice to wedge against an empty spot in a soul that needs refreshed? Getting that done would really take a loaf of Wonder Bread.

Among the Thorns

If first impressions count, it was pretty clear that I did not. The clerk was furious with me.

My family had pulled into the campground on a scorching, summer day and barely found a place to park. Nearly fifty adults surrounded the KOA office, and the parking lot hinted that none had ridden together. That was not true for my girls. It had been a tight fit inside our vehicle and a long ride. Stretching legs and breathing fresh air again was great, but getting into our cabins might take some time.

Fortunately the crowd blocked everything but the registration desk. It was evident that there was a problem. As I walked by, some "what will we do's" were whispered, but I hurried past too quickly to hear an entire conversation. I wondered if someone had forgotten to book a room. Maybe a suggestion would be appropriate.

When the lady at the register asked what she could do for me, I informed her that I had reserved two cabins. In silence she searched through the paper work. There had been no moment during the three hour drive that had been that quiet. I interrupted the stillness with what I thought was a magnanimous gesture of goodwill.

"If you need an extra room, we can make do with one cabin instead of two."

It was then that an emotional reprimand commenced. She must have been someone's sister because she started her lecture with "Listen, mister." My older sibling had done that for as long as I could remember.

"Listen, mister, you asked for two, and you'll pay for two. We get tired of everybody doing this to us." And, so it began, and the fury was unleashed.

Admittedly I was not happy with her tone, especially since I was sure that my sister Linda had a patent on it. Why would she not want one of the other families to have accommodations? But, I bit my tongue, waved off the tirade, and paid for the cabins.

After we unpacked, I walked back to the office for ice. If I had to buy two bags because I was in two cabins, I would. Halfway there, however, the cause of the distress became clear.

A deputy stood beside his patrol car. He pointed and said, "Take your group to the west. Look for places he could crawl into. He couldn't have gone far."

Minutes later I handed Miss Mary Sunshine a few dollars for the ice and asked how long the boy had been missing. Because it would have attracted the kid in me, I checked to see if a playground or railroad tracks were nearby. She offered no smile as she counted out my change, but she did not hesitate to describe the two-year-old blond. The playground was behind the office building, and the tracks were at the end of it. Her sympathy for the family almost made me forgive her for the earlier outburst.

As I opened the screen door, she stressed that the searchers had spent all morning near the swings. After delivering the ice, I headed in that direction anyway. Maybe I went there to irritate her, or maybe I was just escaping from everybody for a moment. Julie laughed at the idea of my looking for the missing boy. At home

I can never find anything without her help. She regularly scolds my lack of focus by saying, "If I am ever lost, I don't want you with the search party."

At the tracks I climbed the gravel incline and sat down. In my youth I had rested on similar iron rails and aimed my slingshot at anything that moved. Sometimes the targets were the stationary, glass insulators on the electric lines that ran parallel to the tracks. An ample supply of rocks let me fire away until I was tired.

Though slight, the elevation made it easy to see everything. The playground had been abandoned. The heat was intense, and parents were keeping their children close at hand for a while. I daydreamed as I watched and listened. I picked up a few stones and tossed them from hand to hand and stared at the landscape. After ten minutes of juggling, a whisper startled me.

It was the sound that a kitten makes, but it was not exactly the sound that a kitten makes. Maybe it was an animal, but it could have been a little kid's cry. I scanned the area again, but nothing was between me and the office. Yet the whimper did not seem to be that far away.

For five minutes I listened and looked. For a moment the sobbing grew louder and distinctively childlike. It came from my left. In the middle of an adjacent plot that had not been mowed, something moved. I tried not to lose sight of the weeds that had tilted ever so slightly as I clambered down from the tracks and walked toward the faint wail.

Thirty feet into the bramble, the child was pinned to the ground by thorns that had snagged his shirt and shorts. Their grip had tightened a little more each time he struggled to free himself. The boy was only visible if someone were standing directly over him. The mass of people that had earlier called out to him would not have heard his weak voice while they were talking. They could not have seen his trapped body from the playground.

After unpinning him, I lifted the toddler, held on dearly, and tramped through prickly plants and aggravating vines. The tears that had streaked through his dirty, sunburnt face stopped as we neared his family. He felt lighter than the berries that had been carried out of the briar patches back home.

Over the years, I think about that little boy on occasion, especially when blackberries and raspberries are ripe. The moist, dark fruits do not look anything like the surrounding green leaves and stems, but sometimes – even when you are standing right next to them – the biggest and brightest of nature's gifts can be nearly impossible to see. It takes some patience and little luck to find the hidden ones, but the effort is worth it.

No Medal

I rarely stayed at home by myself. It just did not happen. We were a family of seven who always had guests. If anything, I remember praying to be alone. That happened in the fields when I drove the tractor. And, it happened one weekend when I was fifteen.

There was no work to be done and no one arguing to watch a different television show. I owned the couch and had little ambition to leave the cushions. Occasionally I got up and twisted the knob to change the channel. It was hardly strenuous and required little thought since we only had five stations to choose from. There were thirteen numbers on the dial, but most were not needed.

For a moment, that afternoon felt right. The phone did not ring, and the reception was good. The guys in the white hats were winning, and I was dosing off. But it was not a peace that would last. Both the movie and my innocence were interrupted by a long, shrill scream.

I looked out the window and witnessed a neighbor running from her trailer and the small television that had been hurled through the air at her head. Her pleas were unintelligible, but the path towards me was clear and certain. From her doorway a man yelled obscenities as she raced across the yard. I was wide awake when the lady reached our back door and he leaped out after her

Suddenly her cries were crystal clear. She shrieked, "He's got a gun."

Gun or no gun, I stumbled, caught my balance, and ran to the front door. The woman was on my heels when I exited and raced around the corner to an unoccupied mobile home. By the time the man started into my house, we had entered the unlocked trailer, bolted the door, and hidden where no one could see us. Thankfully he charged in the opposite direction and towards the truck stop near the highway.

Oddly, I don't know what happened after that. It was as if her eventual departure and my returning home never happened. The rest of the story is a blank. I am as confused today by the loss of those memories as I am by the loss of humanity that leads to acts of abuse and domestic violence. What do victims remember? What do they want to forget?

When I was ten, my cousin Clarence handed me a pistol and let me fire it. Pulling the trigger was easy enough, but the target couldn't have been safer. Despite standing on top of it, the bullet kicked up dirt a yard away. Yet, over the years, that errant shot and the laughter that followed are clearly ingrained in my head.

The can was shiny and had a remnant of the label stuck to it. The only hole in it was where the lid had been removed. So, if I can picture the western handgun and the target, why can't I remember what the women who ran through my house looked like, how long we hid in the trailer, and how I felt about being alone at home afterwards?

Since I don't know what eventually happened, the story has no happy or sad ending; and I am certain that it has no heroes. I only knew that she was behind me because she grabbed my hand as I rushed out of the house and because she was still with me when we hid.

The woman, maybe a fair maiden, was in danger, but no white knight appeared. Fear pushed me out of my comfort zone and through the front door. I had no plan, just the good fortune that an unrented trailer was open and that her angry acquaintance had gone the wrong way.

Adrenaline and luck were effective allies that day, and a boy became an awkward partner. Surely there has to be a better strategy for those in need.

The Eulogy

Aunt Juanita generally wore a big smile and laughed when I saw her, but her demeanor was serious this time.

"Would you do Bob's eulogy?"

When she mentioned it weeks before, the question had caught me off guard. I can't remember if I had uttered the "Let me know what I can do for you" statement or not. If I did, I meant it; but I meant it on my terms. It was like asking:

"Can I mow your lawn?"

"Can I help clean?"

"Can I pick up some groceries for you?"

I was willing to expend time and effort, but giving the eulogy was different. How do you capture a bit of someone's soul in five minutes? I was not sure that I could do him justice but did not hesitate to make the commitment.

My father-in-law has always been so graceful and caring at funerals. For decades I have heard Fred Darling celebrate lives and bring peace to those who paid their final respects. And, I watched him gather information in the days prior to the service as he spoke with one person and then another. He looked for moments that captured the loved one. Those people built the eulogy. As a minister, Fred had a talent for organizing and selecting what best represented the individual who could no longer tell his or her own story.

With that in mind, I visited Aunt Juanita and her sons the evening before the ceremony. We sat in the living room as I asked what they wanted others to know about Bob. I doubt I had ever heard him string more than two or three sentences together at a time. He said little but saw everything.

The most I really knew about him was from his sister. Days before when I had admired the picture of a three-year-old Bob, Betty explained how he got the clothes he was wearing in the photograph. At fourteen, she had worked hard, sold vegetables in Edinburgh, and made enough money to splurge on a nice outfit at Danner's 5 & 10 (five and dime) store for her baby brother. He must have appreciated her attention. Nearly seventy-seven years later and until he was too weak, he called his sister every evening at the same time.

In the past I could not remember hearing my cousins say much about their dad. That changed as one memory followed another. Sincere voices and warm smiles eased the tension in the room. For thirty minutes, they painted a picture of his character.

A man can wear a lot of hats in eighty years. Bob Owens sure did. He was a veteran, a bread winner, a gardener, and a hunter and fisherman. If you walked into his living room, you could see his favorite catches. Mounted fish were on the wall, and Juanita was in her arm chair. He was also a husband, a father, a grandfather, a great-grandfather, a brother, and the youngest of nine children.

He loved his grandkids. He watched them play ball, attended events when he could, and even nicknamed one of 'em "Sap Head" after she tackled a tree and had the sticky substance all over her pretty head afterwards. And, for those of us who knew Bob as an observant listener – not a talker, it was amazing that he called the grandchildren on their birthdays and did not stop singing until he had finished his rendition of "Happy Birthday."

In the Army he had been an MP in Korea and was strongly considered as a guard for the Tomb of the Unknown Soldier. But he had a bigger mission, perhaps a more courageous and demanding commitment to pursue. His "Mission Impossible…should he decide to accept" would be a daunting fifty-year assignment. He was to marry not just Juanita but Juanita and three boys. He had an instant family and a fourth son to add.

He accepted the challenge, and Aunt Juanita sang his praises. "He was a wonderful, caring man who loved his sons and wife." Like their mom, the boys loved and respected him too.

Tony said, "He was a good teacher, especially about hunting and fishing. He would show us how to do it, tell us, and then turn us loose. He expected us to learn." He must have been brave to turn those four loose.

Bob took care of his family. During the blizzard of '78, Steve was employed at Saps, our local donut factory. Columbus was closed, and Steve was stuck at work. The trip to town and back generally lasted a half an hour. Despite the snow and wind, Bob and his trustworthy Nova headed in. It took three and a half hours to get to Saps, pick up Steve and all the pastries that his pockets could hold, and get him back home.

This father of four respected the country he had served. When Ken graduated from the Marine's Embassy Guard School, Bob bought himself and Tony a ticket for an airplane so they could attend the ceremony. In Washington,

D.C., he sat comfortably in a room with senators and generals and congressmen while the most influential men in Washington raised their glasses and toasted him and the other fathers for the contributions they had made to sons and country.

Gary shared a handwritten note:

For as long as I can remember, we have talked every day. The conversation would start "Watcha doin'? Is anybody finding mushrooms? Are the bluegill on the nest? Have you seen any deer?" Never about himself, only everyone else (family, mostly mom). He taught me more than he will know. How to be strong, patient, loving and caring.

They say there are no heroes left, but I know one.

And, the whole family described him as kind and generous. No wonder he had been surrounded by them in his final week. They agreed that he liked to vacation and shared that shortly after the wedding, he and Juanita took the boys to the Wisconsin Dells for an unforgettable experience. It was a magical 'Yes" trip.

"Can we ride the ponies?"
"Yes."
"Can we fish?"
"Yes."
"Can we swim?"
"Yes".

But after days of the never-ending "Yes, you can" the world suddenly turned sour when he responded NO to buying tickets for a helicopter ride just before they left. For an hour or so, he was not forgiven. It wasn't until they reached the Chicago Toll Road booth that the boys understood why that last request had been denied. They watched as Bob and Juanita searched their pockets, the purse, and the car for change for the toll road.

They had enough gas to get home, but not an extra dime to their name. When all seemed lost, Bob took a worn silver dollar from his wallet and paid the fee. It had belonged to his father, and he had carried it for a long time. He used his last dollar, a keepsake, to get his family home.

If you talk to the family that he loved dearly, I believe they will tell you that, for a half century, he gave them all he had. I hear that often about my relatives. I say it often about my parents and siblings.

Nudge Me Gently

Towards Learning Something

A Blue Heron

"I've learned that you shouldn't go through life with a catcher's mitt on both hands; you need to be able to throw something back."

Maya Angelo

The Big Bird of Azalia

In Sandcreek Township secrets were not necessarily prompted by promises or honor or deception ... or any of the stuff that thrillers are made of. Occasionally the necessity for silence came with innocence and a sprinkling of enthusiasm.

Once upon a time, for example, when sci-fi films held me spellbound on Saturday evenings, I believed it was possible to step through the late-night portals to excitement. Those movies depicted a world of gateways. A cave could lead to a hidden valley. Unchartered islands might host lost civilizations. So, it is of little wonder that I developed a boyish zeal for history books and encyclopedias. Surviving a journey into the unknown would demand a great deal of knowledge.

Admittedly, I strayed a bit from reality by over preparing for fantasies and under preparing for everyday experiences. Robin Hood and Daniel Boone were old acquaintances. African animals seemed easy enough to talk to after watching *Bomba the Jungle Boy* and Johnny Weissmuller. But, if I biked through the countryside, I couldn't tell you the difference between any of the breeds of pigs or cows or chickens; and the names of the vehicles that passed me were limited to *car* and *truck* and *station wagon*. Little attention was given to the model and make.

It was in those years that I made one of the most phenomenal discoveries of modern times. Yes, during the glorious days of books and movies, a mere Midwestern boy spotted the last of the pterodactyls when its monstrous silhouette swooped above the trees that lined the banks of White River. My heart pounded as the distant silhouette of the prehistoric form appeared again and then disappeared in almost the same instance. Distracted, I nearly crashed my bicycle in front of Mr. Thomas' turkey farm.

"Heaven help us all," I thought, "if that Jurassic reptile has been courting the Thomas turkeys. Hatching time will be a nightmare."

Jules Verne laid the groundwork for surprise encounters with dinosaurs and giant beasts. *World Book* provided the images. *National Geographic* would have put Azalia on the map if a call had been made. Yet I was not sure that anyone would believe the tale and just as certain that a single sighting by a Walter Mitty personality would carry little weight. My lips, therefore, were sealed.

In the months that followed, carving the main entree at Thanksgiving and Christmas made me uneasy, but I never said a word as I checked the Butterballs for any physical deformities. Neither did I share that I was reading all I could about carnivorous, Stone-Age creatures that could fly. However, I would have broken my vow of silence and notified the authorities immediately if a cow or child had suddenly disappeared...or if a big ole tom had looked at me cross-eyed.

To be honest with you, the reason I kept the secret for a half century is that I lost confidence in the memory when a friend pointed out a Blue Heron standing in a creek bed a year or two later. It might have been the first time I had seen one, but I was not certain. When the long-legged bird launched itself and glided above the sycamores, it reminded me quite a bit of my pterodactyl sighting. The similarity was probably coincidental, but the seeds of doubt were planted.

It might not surprise you that I have always dreamed of discovering something that no one else had found. That particular ambition has made me susceptible to believing in anything the echoes the scripts of *The X-Files* or *The Twilight Zone*. As you know, the truth is out there, and some of it is strange.

Ten years ago, for example, my brother-in-law and I were on a canoe trip when another odd sighting paralyzed my paddle hands. David pointed to the sky where a freak of nature, a hawk with a furry tail glided ahead of us. Once again my heart pounded the adventure rhythm as I searched for Anderson Cooper's number. Luckily, the feathered hunter angled just enough to our left that the squirrel he had caught for lunch was visible. What an amazing sight! Yet had I jumped on the evolution bandwagon and made the phone call, I would have become a part of the food chain too. The reporters would have eaten me alive.

Not all secrets gnaw at my soul or slash with pterodactyl talons when I sleep at night. One or two remind me that the world that still offers tremendous opportunities for unbridled imagination.

The Quiz

"Take out a sheet of paper and number it to twenty," was an atypical request.

Like every other senior in the class, I found a piece of paper, but I also looked for the television crew. Was someone filming a special for *Candid Camera*?

This was the first day of the last English class that I would need to graduate from college, but suddenly it felt more like junior high. Pop quizzes hadn't been announced since I stepped foot on campus. I would not have winced as much if we had been given a pre-class assignment like the one from the foreign language professor. My stomach felt the way it always did when I realized that I had just sped past a patrol car. Surprises have never set well with me.

After only a few questions, I slumped forward in the chair. Where did he find the obscure quotes? Who sits in the library all night remembering every phrase from every book that was ever written? Near the end of the test, most of the class had dropped down in their seats. It was apparent that a diploma might not be within our grasps. The only positive was that my ink was not wasted. I just did not use it. Thirteen blanks, three sure answers, two pretty good guesses and two more opportunity to push my score above twenty percent. I was not going to be the teacher's pet.

Dr. Smith must have pegged us pretty well. Seated in that room was the most unprepared group of future teachers the world had ever seen. The cameraman had to be laughing. When they hoisted the billboard of our class picture, schools across the nation would want the photo. There would be no interviews because no one would hire us.

"Put the paper away," he said as he moved to the left of the room and sat on the desk. "I just wanted your full attention. The truth is that you will never know enough. There will always be a challenge. Keep in mind that if you are satisfied with what you know now, you're in trouble. But, if you become a lifelong learner, you have a chance."

What great insight! Had he just said that in the beginning, the soliloquy would have been written word for word in my notes. He took a deep breath before adding another thought. Undoubtedly the shrewd sage had more wisdom to bestow upon us.

"You might not believe it, but you would do well on this quiz if I asked you to work together to answer the questions. You don't have to know everything, but it is helpful to know who to call on. Recognizing the talents of the people you are with is as important as reading the books."

With that said he started through the test. It was amazing how one student after another buzzed in with an astonishing answer. The junior high feeling was still there. The girls had answered seventeen questions in a row. How could they be so smart? Usually there were benefits when I was the only guy in class but not this time.

No, make it eighteen. The young lady in the back row impolitely shouted out "The Peloponnesian War" before she was called on. That was her third answer, but who was counting? The important thing was that we worked well as a group and that I knew a Miss Manners class that she could enroll in for extra credit.

Dr. Smith moved to the collegiate dictionary. The lexicon was more than a foot thick and filled with a wealth of words that mankind had accumulated and forgotten. He opened it to the middle and started thumbing through the pages as he spoke.

"The final question has two parts. I would have asked you to define and to spell *plenipotentiary*. But, over the years, no class has been able to do either."

He continued to emphasize that we did not know everything and added that, even with help, the answers might elude us. I could feel the I-got-three-right scholar's eyes upon me and knew I had only one chance to justify the existence of the male species.

In an effort to set a good example for her, I raised my hand and politely asked if he minded if I attempted an answer. When he questioned which I would like to try, I said, "Both." He eyed every letter while I waded through the spelling, and his finger underlined the definition as he waited to hear what I had in mind.

The lessons that were shared that day have been invaluable: Don't be satisfied with what you know. When the answer escapes you, trust that someone else might have it. And, all any of us may have is the question. It might be up to the next group to find an effective response. By the way, the fourth thing I took home from that class was a reminder that it doesn't hurt to be lucky.

Vocabulary had never been a strong suit, and spelling was my nightmare. Yet both had motivated me to use the dictionary. The prior evening had been spent reading a German text about Otto von Bismarck. The German word for *plenipotentiary,** his diplomatic status, seemed to blanket an entire line. When I found it, I memorized both the English spelling and the definition.

Dr. Smith made us better classroom teachers before we headed off to be educational ambassadors.

* *plenipotentiary (noun):* a person or diplomatic agent invested with full power to transact business

What's Your Name?

Since the flakes had started down only an hour before school, the sidewalks were not yet cleaned. The slow accumulation reminded me of the snow globe on my desk. When I shook it, the sparkles floated gently and evenly. The weather outside painted a similar, hypnotic scene. The biggest difference was that no footprints marred the rustic setting inside the glass dome.

The first semester would end in two days, but there was still work to be done. Some of my literature students were reading books. Those who had unfinished assignments had an opportunity to catch up. Unfortunately, their current grades reflected a lack of responsibility, not a lack of ability. Too many of my second period students had dug a hole for themselves and had precious little time to climb out. They made no excuses but found a good reason to apply their skills when I pointed out what parents might see on the grade cards.

The knock at the door distracted us. A counselor stood outside with a new student. During the introduction, the young man was unusually quiet. As I provided him an assignment, several scholars lined up anxiously with completed handouts.

When I asked where he had moved in from, he shrugged his shoulders and said, "From the room just below this one."

Prep time finally arrived, and I made a beeline to the office to ask if there was a reason for not waiting until the start of the second semester to transfer him into my class. The counselor shook his head and divulged what had prompted the change.

Snowfall, the end of the semester, too much sugar and caffeine for breakfast.... I am not sure that anyone could explain the cause for the morning disruption in the class he had been in. For the most part it was typical school confusion. There had been too much talking and too little attention to the task at hand. I understood that, and so did many of my pupils who had grown fonder of fellowship than homework.

It took a bit of effort, but his instructor eventually regained some control. Her patience was wearing thin when she called out, "Joe, I asked you to settle down."

Later, she chided, "Joe, I said to get quiet."

The final warning was, "Joe, one more time, and I will take you to the office."

Minutes later, she walked to the back of the room to escort the talkative student to the office. The report that she dragged him by the ear may have been exaggerated. Allegedly she had held so firmly that his feet barely touched the tiles.

"My name's not Joe," echoed down the hallway and into the office. His defense had some merit though it did not excuse the loquacious behavior. He was certain that he was the victim of an injustice.

I am as forgetful as anyone. Names just escape me. When I meet a person that I have not seen for a while, I might start with the universal name of choice as I fumble for the one on the birth certificate. An easy stall is "YOU look great. How have YOU been?" Julie might tell YOU that I called her by the wrong name when we started dating, but the mistake did not continue for eighteen weeks. His previous literature teacher must have had a lot on her mind that day.

In the story of Rumpelstiltskin, knowing a name saved a child and kept a family together. I cannot tell you how often that actually happens, but I am sure that it does at times. When someone remembers my name, I feel welcomed. I feel like I have a reason to be there. Our students need the same recognition and encouragement too.

Nearly a thousand people entered the middle school that morning. The sidewalks bore the impressions of boots and shoes and slide marks. I could not identify the student who made it, but the one who created the snow angel might have had wet pants. The one whose name had been forgotten slipped into my class.

The Weakest Link

Keith Mitchell loved Northside track. He must have needed an assistant pretty badly the day he knocked on my classroom door. I agreed to help because Jim Maple, our athletic director, had always said, 'It's just natural. You can always find a kid who can run and jump and throw." Besides, I knew how to take attendance and collect physical forms.

Some truly gifted athletes come out that year, and Keith knew how to get them ready. He had designed more ways to stretch the body than anyone I knew. If the Inquisition had required track instead of the rack, one of Keith's ancestors might have been the coach. The first ten days we stretched for an hour and practiced the events for only thirty minutes because it was a part of "the plan."

However, we hit a snag the third week. Keith came down with something awful, as did Lee Bridges who ran like a cheetah. Since it was almost impossible to cover the roster and the one hundred and ten exercises before the parents picked up their kids, some changes were made. I finally decided that I could call roll, do some of the warm ups, and then blow the whistle to send them off to their field events and running assignments. The shrill blast put the young men in charge.

Both Coach Mitchell and Lee returned just before the first meet. Lee shattered the school record in the 400 and lowered it even more when he got his strength back. Coach grinned as he clocked the race.

"I knew those practice plans were good," he said as he checked the stopwatch.

At the time I did not have the heart to tell him that I was not smart enough to follow his warm-up manual or that Lee had been at home in bed. What I do know is that they were both very talented. Lee won two state titles in high school and earned All-American honors in college. In track and field Keith was nationally recognized for his officiating skills.

Another mentor who shared his knowledge with me was Neil Reed. For a while Neil had coached with Adolf Rupp. At Kentucky he recruited players who would win a national title, and then he assisted John Wooden at UCLA. Later he taught with me at the junior high in Jennings County. Surprisingly, Neil also put his reputation on the line and let me coach the Panthers too.

One weekend we were assigned to scout a game for the high school team. I looked professional carrying the clipboard through the gate, but Neil had a mind for strategy. After five minutes, he told me to relax. He then called the next ten plays in a row before the offense left the huddle. He was at a whole different level in his grasp of sports.

Football was a little like track. You can always find a kid who can run and jump and throw. When you add a few who can kick and hit and catch, you have a team. Our squad had a little of everything, but we got crushed at the line.

"These are great kids. They do everything we ask. What's our problem?" Neil was truly frustrated or he would not have tapped into my vast wealth of football savvy.

My immediate response was something like, "Our linemen's average weight is ninety-five pounds. Our opponents average over one hundred and fifty."

Neil did not like that. He thought mental toughness and heart could add an extra forty to our totals. His coaching would take care of the other fifteen pounds. I appreciated that about Neil. He expected his team to be in the game.

Well, he had friends who could do more than just read a weight scale, so that evening he sought advice from Homer Rice, a future coach of the Cincinnati Bengals. Homer suggested that we look for bigger boys or accept that there would be some losses. It would not surprise me if Neil had tried to negotiate a trade to upgrade our front line.

Later we gained momentum after the team asked us to watch the lunch-hour, pick-up game. They were keenly aware of their own weaknesses and their own strengths. They were fast but not big.

After a plate lunch and an extra carton of milk the eighth graders ran their legs off with reverses and some razzle-dazzle flea flickers. Those boys had a vision for the field and a faith in each other that was fun to watch. They talked us into adding a couple of their plays. Neil was so right. Heart and coaching, theirs and his, made us look a little bigger on the field.

At the banquet, I did not hide how difficult it was to coach a sport that I had never played. Eventually I thanked the team and the parents for their patience and guidance, and I began with an honest confession.

"When the season started, I didn't know much about football."

From the back of the room a great truth rang out.

"Well, nothing has changed." The laughter that followed was thunderous.

Faith in young people and in those I work with has carried me time and again. The occasional shout from the back of the room has prompted me to work to get better.

Ringside Advice

On one side of me was an Olympic champion. On the other stood an ambitious teenager. The three of us leaned against the ropes that separated the spectators from the wrestling competition. The consolation and championship matches were in progress.

"See those trophies over there. I'm gonna win me one of them trophies. Next year I'll be the champion. Next year that trophy's gonna be mine."

The redhead was stout. His body bounced as he responded to the excitement. He swayed back and forth and shared his dreams aloud. It was no secret that he wanted to be a champion. As he continued to lay claim to a glory that he had not yet won, his hands tightened around the rope, but his eyes struggled. Sometimes he watched the matches, but mostly he eyed the awards. Positioned near the medal stands, he had a good view of both.

At first, he made me laugh, but after his fourth or fifth claim to a future victory, I was not as amused. He reminded me of an old cartoon character, a mouse named Jabber, who annoyingly ranted on and on without inhaling or exhaling.

When the boy finally paused for air, Coach Blubaugh turned to share some guidance. Mr. Blubaugh's neck was thick, but the lens of his glasses might have thicker. The direct gaze and slow delivery captured the athlete's attention when the Olympian spoke.

"Son, I have wrestled all over the world, and I have won. I can't tell you about the trophies. I don't remember them, but I can tell you about the men I faced and the battles. It's about learning to compete. It's about not giving up."

In Rome, Doug Blubaugh was an Olympic wrestling champion. Shelby Wilson, another gold medalist in 1960, had described him to me as "stronger than an acre of garlic." He was still a physical presence and a great technician, but that afternoon he set aside style and strategy and offered insight into what winners are made of.

"I remember the work," he continued, "and the athletes who made me work. I remember the matches, not the medals. Do you know what I'm trying to say?"

"Thank you," the young man said quietly and nodded to confirm that he understood the advice. He extended a hand to Coach Blubaugh.

Afterwards our attention returned to the action on the mats. Yet with his grip tightening on the rope and the bounce back in his legs, the grappler was again overpowered by his desires. He pointed at the awards table and chanted his intentions.

"See those trophies over there. I'm gonna win me one of them trophies. Next year I'm gonna win me one."

Post Holes and Horace

Some of my friends are tremendous storytellers. John Quick and Al Reed have a knack for it, but few others match Don Robertson. He occasionally stops by the office for conversation and fellowship. The room is crowded because he brings a myriad of memories and jokes and thoughts.

Don directed high school bands until his retirement. Television and radio may have missed a potential star. He has that Alex Trebek look and a comedian's timing, but he offers more than one liners. Current events, family, politics, and religion .... He stays in touch with what is happening around him and with what is going on inside himself.

Don has great stories, but most are his to share. His life has joys and successes and challenges and tragedies just like yours and mine. He has met Art Linkletter and Bob Hope and thousands of young people and families. The Shriners Hospital in St. Louis owns a special spot in his heart. But, in my office we often talk about the moments that others may have forgotten. Don does not forget.

He treasured and trusted his grandfather. His respect eased the tension and frustration that occasionally cropped up on the farm. That was especially true when Don was assigned to build a fence around the fields. It was a job that would take all summer.

Having started a few postholes myself, I assure you that the best man for digging is always someone else. Unless the process involves a tractor and an auger, it is a job that no one aspires to have.

Don never elaborated much on the details. A fence row needed little explanation, and the physical aches and pains required even less, especially when he implied that he had hundreds of posts to bury. My shoulders and arms hurt as I listened.

At one point, he was working near the road and, as he said, was feeling pretty sorry for himself. He leaned on the post-hole digger with his head down and debated how the task would ever make a difference in his life.

The car that approached may not have delivered the answer he wanted, but the man behind the wheel gave him something to think about. The elderly driver spied the tormented teen and sensed the dilemma. He parked his car on the berm of the road and approached Don.

"Son," he started. "I'd share some advice if you're willing to listen."

He then recited, "A job dreaded, once started, is half done."

The observant passerby echoed a bit of Horace. Two thousand years before Don dug his first hole, the poet had written, "Dimidium facti, qui coepit, habet; sapere aude, incipe." (He who has begun is half done; dare to know, dare to begin!)

Nearly sixty years later, Don Robertson still carries those words. Sometimes when the workload seems heavy and my self-pity is surging, I signal for that old man pull off on my side of the road. When I am ready to listen, he shares the same wisdom.

Nudge Me Gently

Towards Family

(In alphabetical order)

Fred and Shirley Darling – Julie's parents

Lester and Lillie Perkinson – my parents

"A family is a unit composed not only of children but of men, women, an occasional animal, and the common cold."

Ogden Nash

The Gatherings

When I was a boy, we gathered in the yard outside my grandparent's kitchen. Some owned a seat on the wooden swing. A few rested on the ground, and others stood. One or two leaned against the shade tree, but Grandpa squatted and whittled. On a Saturday or Sunday, a neighbor might drive down the gravel road and easily spot three generations of the Petty clan on that hillside.

Uncles Max and Jack and Jimmy shared the latest news and told tall tales, but almost everyone joined in at one time or another. It's funny, but I don't remember Grandpa saying much. He watched attentively as he shaved through the bark and into the stick that was in his left hand. Sharpening and re-sharpening it seemed to relax him as he listened. I imagine that he did the same thing when he sat under a tree during squirrel season.

In my twenties, I bought a pocket knife with the intent of perching on the front porch of the farmhouse and cutting on a piece of wood. A Barlow would have been cheaper, but the guy behind the counter assured me that it was not as sharp as the knife I bought. That evening I picked up a branch, snapped off a foot-long section, and started slicing on it and inadvertently on my thumb. I am glad no one was there to take a picture of the five band aids that eventually patched the fingers on my left hand.

Rather than forfeit any body parts, I gave up on whittling that very night; but meeting with family has remained an important part of my life. The need to congregate seems embedded in the Perkinson-Petty genetics. A wedding brings us together. A funeral musters the forces. And, heaven help the waiting room if one of us is in the hospital. The truth be told, if two or more of us are together, the rest of the family may show up for the occasion.

My friend Chris Kimmerling also came from a large family that had the Let's-Get-Together chromosome. When she first described her reunions, the events were immense with relatives lined up like rows of corn when the food was ready. Years later, a generation of both our clans has been harvested and another has been born to embrace the rewards of kinship.

There was little grass where we assembled on the Petty farm. The ground was worn from use and trampled by fellowship. To this day I cannot drive through the Henryville area without remembering the acquaintances of my youth and seeing a pair of old hands shaving away on a stick. He carved that image in my mind as well. My family stamped the need for the gatherings in my soul.

Home Improvement

The North Vernon apartment that Julie and I first lived in was on the second floor above a refinishing business. It sat across the street from the middle school where I taught. On muggy nights an unbearable heat settled in every room since we had no air conditioner. On weekends, when the cars raced at the nearby track, the rumble of engines echoed off the walls and made life even more uncomfortable. Once or twice we spent Friday and Saturday with Julie's parents.

But, all in all, having a place of our own was wonderful. I could walk to school and be home soon afterwards. We had enough for groceries but budgeting for fuel would have required tightening our already tightened belts. On the Thursdays before pay day, when the gas tank registered empty and the cupboard was bare, we walked two miles across town to a restaurant and wrote a check for a feast. Fortunately, banking was not as instant as it has become in today's world. Our earnings were deposited the next day and always got there ahead of the dinner check.

The enclosed stairway to the apartment was drab and worn. Wanting to make a good impression on our guests, I picked up some paint. Before I opened the can or found the brush, I spent a few evenings prepping for the final touches. By Sunday afternoon the warm weather seemed perfect, so I stirred the oil paint and let Julie know that we would be shut in for the evening. There was no doubt in my mind that it would dry overnight.

The original plan was to coat every other step. I would start at the top and work my way down. Once at the bottom, the can would be sealed and the brush would be wrapped in a plastic bag to keep it from drying out. The unpainted sections would be finished the following evening. Hindsight tells me that I should not have discarded that idea, but a beautiful summer sky said, "Go ahead."

It was warm. A gentle breeze fanned the heat but did not blow the dust. The temperature seemed so right that I decided to paint it all. I tacked a "Do Not Enter" sign to the outside of the street-level entrance and left the door slightly ajar so that the air would circulate and fan the paint. Because of the optimal conditions, I started at the bottom and worked my way to the top. Every step and every inch of the stairway was covered with a smooth, glossy finish.

Like a contortionist I bent backwards and moved sideways up to the kitchen entry before the sun went down. The wood glistened. The aqua blue paint brightened the stairwell. Visitors would feel welcomed before they were ever greeted at the upstairs door.

Unexpectedly a sharp roll of thunder announced a storm as soon as I had cleaned the brush. The once gentle breeze turned into a fierce gust, and the dry heat that had defined the day was chased away by a wall of rain. Under the streetlights, the luster of the puddles matched the sheen that reflected off the steps. I knew I was in trouble. Even worse, Julie knew it too.

The next morning I opened the door and checked my handiwork. Since moisture was not an ally of oil-based products, the paint looked just as wet as it had in the can. The door that had been left open at the bottom had not helped either. And there we stood. Julie was pregnant, and I was dressed for school. Both of us had places to go and possibly no way to get there.

Because it seemed like the right thing to say, I promised her that I would have a solution as soon as the school day ended. Then I held her in my arms and savored the warmth of a kiss as I had seen those heroes of the big screen do. Well, maybe I just asked her not to be too mad and walked to the window that faced the alley. I slid it up, leaned out, and grabbed a branch of the tree that had been growing for years for just this moment. Swinging to the middle of the maple, I climbed from limb to limb until it was safe enough to drop to the ground. I did not look back at the mother-to-be of my first born.

It is altogether possible that I did not say a word to anyone at school about my predicament. I did, however, glance across the street from time to time to see what was going on in the kitchen. I feared that Julie had been sharpening knives all afternoon.

At the end of the school day the steps looked better, but they were still too sticky to walk on. Julie might have slipped or fallen. Depending on her mood, she might have pushed me on my way. Not wanting either to happen, I purchased a carpet remnant and some small nails. It took an hour or more, but I eventually cut out rectangles and tacked one on the top of each step. It looked like that was what we had intended to do all along.

Afterwards we left the vapors and our apartment for a while. Surprisingly, Julie came back with me that evening. Her home improvement plan has generally included finding a touch of character in each of our homes and accepting the character she lives with.

Love the Fair

Fairground events have always been source of amusement and fellowship. I've sold popcorn at a rodeo fundraiser, burgers at the demolition derby, and once chipped all evening on a bucket of frozen, Coney-dog sauce for the D.A.R.E. chuck wagon. Whether I was there for presentations or entertainment, I rarely left without a story.

One of my first dates with Julie was to the county fair. We walked for miles and wandered round and round the midway. In the years that followed, stops for lemon shakeups and elephant ears were highlights, but that first evening was spent circling the path that led to the rides and the ring tosses and the guess-my-weight booth.

The crowd and the dust were equally thick. The roar from the grandstand races and the constant barking of the carnies blended with the music and neon signs. But, of all the sounds that night, the most memorable was the frustration of the mom who lifted her child in front of her for some stern advice.

"If you soil your britches one more time, we're going home," is the paraphrased version of her edict. Since wisdom like that is worth remembering, her declaration would later become a standard rule in our household.

Years later, one of my first-year students collected tickets and managed a spinning contraption that all the risk takers lined up for. Once he checked the seatbelts and started the ride, I walked over to say hello. I was curious about the cast on his arm and the one on his leg.

"Well, I was at the park in North Vernon, and a guy bet me five dollars that I couldn't ride my bike over this ledge and jump to the other side of the creek. It was a ten foot drop and a ten foot jump. I should have taken him for more money. I made it but wrecked my bike."

He was more of a daredevil than I remembered but a poor financier. Evel Knievel would have haggled for the additional funding. The sling did not look comfortable and neither did the crutch. It must have hurt a lot when he crashed into the embankment.

For the reception we rented one of the fairground buildings for Charity's wedding. *What a Wonderful World* played for the father-daughter dance, and I honored the moment by not stepping on her dress. Louie Armstrong sang, "And I think to myself/What a wonderful world," and I thought it would be if I didn't smash her toes.

Unfortunately when it was time for the ever popular *Chicken Dance*, a rubber rooster hat was ceremoniously placed on my head. Our friend Alan Trisler found way too much humor in orchestrating the moment.

A few buildings down from us a crowd was filing in to watch a professional wrestling match that same night. Our group was bigger, but the ticket holders for the bouts looked meaner. Had a melee erupted, my people would literally have lost their shirts. Actually, I might have recouped the reception expenses if I had suited up and donned the chicken headgear. I could have competed under the alias of Rooster Boy or worn it as I sold our extra wedding desserts to the bleacher crowd.

As I watched Charity on the dance floor, my mind drifted back to the summer that had followed her birth. Julie and I did what young parents are apt to do. We paraded our daughter at the fair. It was so wonderful. Unlike the teens who accompanied their parents, baby Charity did not ask for money or for one more ride or to walk around with her friends instead of us.

The intent of the procession was to show off a beautiful, newborn girl. Friends and strangers expressed compliments. The sheep baaed, and the cows mooed when she passed by. Now they did that when just about anyone walked through the barn, but I could hear a special tone in their greeting for her. After visiting the exhibits, we decided to walk the midway at least once. As always, it was packed.

I carried Charity to give Julie a chance to feast on a corn dog and coke. We walked beside each other for a while, but eventually the crowd separated us. Julie tried to catch up, but like Persephone she moved in silence. Concerned that nothing had been said for a while, I turned around just as she tapped my shoulder. Her cheeks were blue, and her hand was at her throat. People watched the flashing lights and the Ferris wheel and looked for friends. But, her choking appeared to have gone unnoticed.

There was no place to set a baby, so I held Charity in one arm and backhanded her mother's sternum with the knuckles of my right fist. Corn dog and ice flew everywhere. Julie gasped for air as the color returned to her face.

To my surprise, one old man had apparently witnessed the entire crisis and knew why she had been slugged. He commented matter-of-factly, "I never seen it done like that before. I wondered what you would do."

As soon I was sure that Julie was okay, I amended the family rule that we had borrowed to include choking. I told her, "If you do that one more time, we are going home."

Bewitched

Julie and I had been over every inch of the nursery. Once and then twice the end-of-the-season specials were examined. After weighing the pros and cons of this flower or that one, we asked ourselves if any of the shrubs were really a good match for our needs. Eventually we bought a stick. Sure it had a label that said it was a Japanese maple, a dwarf red maple, but it looked more like a puny version of the Charlie Brown Christmas Tree.

That fall the scrawny sapling was planted near the back corner of the garage. Black-Eyed Susans and the tree that might someday rise just above them outlined a mulched hideaway that Hannah could escape to when she was big enough to go outside on her own.

Four years later, the plants thrived, and our youngest had grown into an imaginative sprite. Since the cone flowers were still colorful in late September, a wall of yellow blooms surrounded a wooden bench that Hannah and I had made. Their golden tint contrasted beautifully with the fragile, scarlet leaves of the maple.

When I pulled in the driveway, I could see Luke and Andy and Hannah huddled together. The two blondes and our red head blended into the scenery, but it was obvious that something was being energetically stirred in an aluminum bowl. Squatted next to the Japanese maple, the children laughed as they worked. They were so involved that they did not hear my approach.

The unexpected left me speechless for a moment. I fought to mask my horror when I realized that six little hands were cramming hundreds of leaves into the container. They had pulled them from the Japanese maple.

Dumbfounded, I finally asked, "What are you doing?"

Not embarrassed to be sitting next to a tree that had been stripped naked, they exclaimed in unison, "Making magic!"

How could they not be? They had found the Tree of Resilience, a twig that had survived. They had plucked the delicate, seven-pointed leaves and were making a potion from what must have looked like Faerie stars to them. It was a powerful concoction with a mojo that was strong enough to save the children and eventually the tree.

I don't know which parent provided the abracadabra gene for Luke and Andy Carr, but Hannah and my girls inherited it from Julie. She does not need bat wings or eye of newt to conjure up her unique brand of delight. She wields spontaneity and youthful charm like a sorceress uses incantations.

A few years before, for example, we were shopping at the Wal-Mart in Seymour when darkness canceled sunshine and crashing thunder announced a menacing squall. Neither Julie nor any of the other customers had anticipated the need for umbrellas or the deafening sheets of rain that pounded the roof.

Twenty minutes later a steady downpour replaced the gales, and an entrance full of customers blocked our departure. The storm was passing, but it had left the parking area flooded. Julie tugged at my hand and pulled me through the crowd and toward the door.

"Come on. We haven't walked in the rain in a long time," she coaxed.

Noah would have been in trouble if his wife had made the same suggestion, but this was not the end of the world. We did not roll up our pants, take off our shoes, or cover our heads. Instead we waded leisurely to our car and enjoyed the moment.

Behind us, several couples enviously whispered, "That looks like fun."

We need the delight of magic leaves and puddles, even parking-lot puddles, in our lives. More importantly, we need a friend to share them with.

Too Lenient

I am not an indoor-pet lover. Never have been. Doubt that I ever will be. But, occasionally I have indulged my daughters. Gold fish from the county fair overstayed their welcome. More than once, a fragile puppy was sneaked into the house. Somehow the tiny dogs survived the little girls and all the squeezes that came with outstretched arms. Then each would grow strong enough to chew through rugs and curtains and my tennis shoes.

Finally I laid down the law and said that no more creatures with claws, paws, or sharp teeth could stay with us. Now I am, however, better at making rules than enforcing them. So, when our twenty-two year old recently visited for the weekend and brought her apartment kitty, both were afforded hospitality.

Hannah dubbed the ebony beast with a warrior's name, but I called him Sylvester as a reminder that he was just a "puddy cat." Despite my belittling remarks, his courage was evident. With absolutely no warning he would boldly pounce on inanimate objects that could not fight back.

That cat walked thin with his youthful frame stretching just enough to get in my way. Like most felines, he sensed who liked him least and taunted the individual by constantly rubbing against his leg or by walking just beneath his feet. I was irritated but did find it amusing when he arched like the cats in Halloween drawings that can stand over pumpkins without touching them.

Well, Sylvester left two days later, but his bathroom set-up did not. It had been emptied on a regular basis, but our guest may have used the facility before his departure. You can imagine my surprise when I awoke from a short winter's nap to find the fourth-grade granddaughter in the kitchen. Because she did not appreciate the aroma that had settled in her playroom, she was cleaning and washing the equipment.

She had poured the sand-like, absorbent litter down the garbage disposal. The dirty, litter-box scoop was soaking in the sink along with the baking utensils and lunch plates. Clay-like debris floated on top of the warm, sudsy water. Some of it was stuck to the pancake flipper that she had used to scrape off the scoop. The only Joy in the house was the bottle of dishwashing detergent that laughed at me from the window ledge.

Two hours later the disposal was cleared, the sanitized scoop and litter box were stored in the garage, and all the dishes were scrubbed three times once I found the bleach. Situations like this explain why I wash the pots and pans at home and do not ask for assistance. I may not be king of the house, but I am the self-appointed Lord of the Sink. I, and only I, am allowed to put anything down the garbage disposal or into the hot, soapy water.

Just to be clear, I prefer outdoor pets, and I have some old rules that need to be posted.

Pledges

When the flag appeared on the television screen, our first and second grade granddaughters jumped up from the couch. Standing as tall as little girls can stand, they placed a hand on their hearts and began in unison:

"I pledge allegiance to the Flag of the United States of America, and to the Republic for which it stands, one Nation under God, indivisible, with liberty and justice for all. Have a happy Wednesday!"

Francis Bellamy's 1892 composition was spoken earnestly. Ryleigh and Claire had it memorized. Their eyes did stray from the red, white, and blue image until the *"Have a happy Wednesday!"* which was what Principal Heiny followed the pledge with each week before the students took their seats.

Mrs. Heiny must have sold warmth with her welcoming challenge. That sentence was recited in such an amiable tone and accompanied by smiles as both young ladies dropped back down on the cushions. They glanced up to see if we were proud of their performance.

My granddaughters may not have entirely understood the meaning of the pledge, but they knew that they were saying something important. Isn't that what rituals do? Ceremonies give us a phrases and actions to capture the essence of a moment or allegiance. The trouble is that we may not quite know what we have caught or committed to.

Forty years ago Julie Darling wore a white dress with lavender trim that her mother made, and I donned a blue blazer and white slacks and clip-on bow tie. We stood in front of her father who officiated the wedding. I don't know if he was as nervous as I was, but he had to be suspect of my potential.

The recollections of that day are a little fuzzy. We stood before family and friends and made all sorts of solemn pledges that would be tested by time. "Do you, Larry, take Julie ... to have and to hold from this day forward ... for better or for worse, for richer, for poorer ... in sickness and in health ... to love and to cherish."

"From this day forward until death do you part?" My head spins when I contemplate the vows. We were young and invincible and in love. We had dreams and the world ahead of us. And yet, we exchanged rings despite the foreboding phrases. Sure, good possibilities (better, richer, richer, health) were emphasized, but the bad ones hinted at tougher times (worse, poorer, sickness). My young-man bravado assured me that we could dodge the bad forever. Fortunately for me, Julie may not have fathomed what she was agreeing to.

Afterwards I signed a county document that may yet come back to haunt me. I believe that I affirmed that I was of "sound mind." There I was with a beautiful lady. I had kissed her in front of God and everybody. I would have made any promise if it meant I could take her home that night. Was I rational or irrational?

The scales must have teetered back and forth on that one. Under all that pressure, I doubt that I was of sound mind, but unless they were requiring a doctor's signature, I was close enough. And, four decades later, my statement about sanity has not yet annulled the contract.

The other day, I asked, "Julie, what do you think has kept us together for all these decades?"

As quickly as she had once said "I do," she responded, "We're both too stubborn to admit we were wrong."

Then she smiled. At least I think it was a smile.

Nudge Me Gently

Towards Some Soul Searching

April Louise and the doll Aunt Amy made her
-    A painting by her Grandmother Shirley Darling
                                                                    -

**"Moral: All men should strive to learn
before they die
what they are running from, and to, and why."**

James Thurber, *The Shore and the Sea*

Let the Records Show

I doubt my kids ever made enough trips to the library, probably because I could never find the card. When we did go, there were two entries to choose from. On the first floor, row after row of big-people books and the checkout staff greeted us. If we were running late for story time or only visiting the children's section, we took the steps to the lower level.

Our girls would either enter like debutantes or like tumblers. They might step delicately as if they were balancing plates on their heads, or they might roll and push and race. The quality of the entrance was important. It would have been no surprise if Marian the Librarian had raised a "10" and awarded the trio golden bookmarks. But, the ceremony would have been delayed since one of the little ladies was always in the restroom.

On one occasion I read them a book that had been left at our table. The artwork colorfully depicted a city park on an active, October day. It started with a leaf falling from a branch. It ended when the leaf hit the ground. In between, the pictures and script depicted the activities that took place. Each page painted a different story with a separate cast of animals and children and families.

Since there were no read-it-again requests, I closed the book. While they went for armloads of tales about princesses and unicorns, I thumbed back through it on my own.

As simple as it was, that story truly captured a part of what happens in real life. So many things are always going on around us. We will not see them all, and we will not remember

all of what was seen. In fact, in only a moment –
maybe no longer than the time it takes for a leaf
to drop from a tree and hit the ground, our
decisions may become a part of someone's
memory. We are not in charge of what others
will say about us in the years to come, but we
certainly may be measured by their perceptions.

At a conference I was fortunate enough to
hear Victor Vieth advocate for the prevention of
child abuse, and I was caught off guard by the
power of a story he told about the First Regiment
of Minnesota. At Gettysburg a plaque
commemorates their valor.

During the battle the Confederate troops
spotted a weakness in the Union defense.
General Winfred Scott Hancock, a career U.S.
Army officer, reacted immediately and asked his
volunteer infantry to hold the compromised
position against much greater odds. He needed
enough time for reinforcements to bolster the
line. His men bought precious minutes and
then some but paid a heavy price. Eighty-two
percent were killed or wounded, but their
sacrifice may have determined the outcome of
the war.

Most of us will not be called upon to give
our lives for a cause, yet there will always be
those who will sacrifice daily for their families
and friends. Ultimately, I'd like to think that
everyone is destined for a moment of purpose. It
may or may not be planned, but we will be
judged by how we face what lies before us.
Truthfully, we won't know if someone might
witness what we do and share that observation
for a lifetime.

Obviously we won't always notice the
leaves that fall gently around us, but we should

111

take advantage of the time that elapses before they land and embrace even the smallest opportunities that are available.

Ambushed

A flat-roofed shed sat on the hill above Grandpa's house, but I have no idea what it was for.   Behind it lay the dense woods that led to squirrel-hunting territory.   A hundred yards in, a ravine sloped to the west towards the county road.   Fallen trees crisscrossed the gap.

One afternoon cousin Bobby and I climbed the ladder that leaned against the back of the shed and walked halfway across the roof to inspect a wasp nest.   The mudded cone hung from a limb that arched above the only entrance. We were close enough to examine it but distant enough to avoid disturbing the dwelling.   It was a learning experience right up to and including the moment that Bobby's brother Andy sneaked up and threw a corncob at the wasps.

Responding to a direct hit on their home, a buzzing horde flew out the hole, but we were almost as fast as they were.   Since the ladder was too far away, we jumped off the structure and ran for our lives.   For a while, the wasps chased us as we chased Andy down the hill.

Later, no one was really mad.   Andy's had pitched a perfect strike.   The wasps were gloriously furious. And, only Butch Cassidy and the Sundance Kid ever made a more perilous leap.   Admittedly we were jealous of bites that looked bigger than our own, but it was not an emotion that festered for days.

Andy grew up to be a bit of a recluse, so I was surprised to hear from him when he left a message last spring.   He had something to talk about and preferred to have the discussion at lunch.   As is often the case, his jovial nature masked the seriousness of his intent.   In a different way, he was about to ambush me again.

Andy had vanished from the family for periods of time since high school, but his stories let us know that he never disappeared from life. He has been a minister and a school bus driver in North Carolina. Factory work had paid the bills. When his housing offered no indoor plumbing, he carried water from the creek. For at least a decade he participated in tribal gatherings and sweat lodge rituals. But, his diabetes had slowed him down, and there were other concerns these past few years.

Soup by Design, a downtown restaurant, was a favorite of his, so we met there. Andy led the way and explained how to order. There were multiple pots of homemade soups. He vouched that each was delicious but would not recommend one over the other. After adding the bread and cookie and drink, we found a table.

Years earlier a friend had commented, "You know you're with family when you break bread together." It felt like Andy and I had done this often. I was glad I came with an appetite, but it was evident that he was hardly hungry. He came to ask a favor, not to eat.

Andy's health had been fragile. Even though he had no pressing concerns, he knew his condition could change without notice. When we were kids, seeing him throw that corncob at the wasp nest was a jaw-dropper. I was just as surprised when I realized that we were meeting to lay the foundation for his funeral. I spooned another bite and picked up a cracker as he talked about what he wanted to happen after he died.

The grin never left his face. He was in no hurry to leave this world, but there had already been too many tomorrows that seemed out of reach for him. He emphasized that he was at peace with his life and with God. He chuckled and explained what he definitely did not want. He smiled as he said that there would be no need for a casket and explained where his ashes should be scattered.

We sat at the table long after my bowl was empty. His insight and rustic wisdom were refreshing. I envied how contently he spoke about his life and how freely he expressed his love for so many people.

Monsters

Grandpa's farm was not hidden, but it was isolated. On a clear night the moon and stars sparkled above it, but his neighbors' lights were blocked by hills and woods.

During the day, there was a clear view of the corncrib and the storage buildings. An iron kettle sat just beyond the summer kitchen that had not been used for years. When our youngest sister Lynnette was born, Gene and I fought cousins Bobby and Andy behind that very kitchen. Although it did not determine the outcome, we exchanged ineffective blows to prove who would be her brothers.

The pigs were fenced in a lot beyond the field that was behind the outhouse. All across the yard, hens and roosters scratched at the earth. On the other side of the gravel road the horse and cow grazed near the creek that ran through the pasture.

Back home the rumbling of highway traffic and the constant sound of neighbors filled the air, but at the farm crickets chirped and birds whistled and Lady barked. It was not necessarily louder, but it was more foreign than I was accustomed to. The screens in the open windows did not muffle the noise or defend against the forest demons that might crawl in.

At Grandpa's, entertainment did not have a price tag, but it required some leg work. We often walked the railroad tracks to the Underwood store and explored the woods as if no one had gone before us. Sometimes we fished or made our own bows and slingshots. Occasionally we grabbed a bar of soap and washed in the bend of the creek where the water was waist deep. Cleanliness might be next to godliness, but our baths were over if a snake poked his head above the waterline.

When the sun faded, we read comic books or played Rook with Aunt Nell. And, there was a black and white television. The picture was a little fuzzy, but the sound was good. I sat in front of it one weekend and watched Clayton Moore in the origin of Lone Ranger. All in all, it was a balanced-enough world. There were good guys and bad ones. That might explain why I also saw evil incarnate gazing straight at me from that very screen.

It was pitch-black outside; and, just as it did each evening, the unknown crept brazenly close to the house and taunted me. The bird dog's sporadic yelps made me nervous. I opened a comic and tried to concentrate on something other than my fears.

That particular evening, I sat with a dozen comic books on my lap. Bobby and Andy and Grandpa watched television with me as the show introduced a horrible witch whose heart was darker than her wardrobe. Her voice was unpleasant and her hair unkempt. She did not shout, "I'll get you my pretty" like Dorothy's nemesis, but she might as well have. Instead she stared at me. I glanced down to avoid the glare; but when I looked up again, her eyes pierced into mine.

Lady roared fiercely as she fended off a nocturnal intruder, and I could have sworn that a twig snapped outside the window behind me. Too afraid to turn around, I checked the room to see if anyone else was concerned, but they were under the influence of the same witch that terrified me.

It was too much. I raised the magazine in front of my face and blocked the monster. When a commercial started, I lowered the book but kept it ready. She would not steal my soul. The Two-Gun Kid would not let her.

But, the fates were crueler than I could ever have suspected that night. The old hag did not harm me. Instead Grandpa caught me hiding from her. As I lowered the western, he grinned. Not a word was said, but he knew I was afraid. I appreciated the courtesy but would have given anything to have kept the secret from him.

The next day I made a promise that I have not been able to keep. I vowed never to be afraid of anything again. Although I do not shiver at dusk or think that the boogeyman lives in the shadows, I have my fears.

I don't believe in monsters as much as I once did and try not to create them as often. After all, making monsters is a dangerous business. Once the label is applied, someone feels obligated to get rid of the designated evil. It is far too easy to hate whatever makes us uncomfortable.

There are still times when I catch myself inventing blame beasts to explain the bad things that happen. However, I no longer sit with the stories of Kid Colt or one of his compadres clutched in my hand. I try not to close my eyes or hide behind a book. Just in case Grandpa is watching, I don't want to be caught cowering from the moments that bother me. Hopefully I have the strength to face the battle at hand.

Grandpa might grin at that too.

What If

Did you ever cover your bases by investing in something that you had little faith in? You might have wished upon a falling star or mistakenly upon the taillights of a plane shooting across the dark sky. Maybe you kept an old rabbit's foot in your pocket even though the bunny's misfortune was obvious.

Since it is bad luck to pick up a penny if it is face down, I have kicked a lot of them until they flipped over and the copper image of old Abe was plain to see. There is a chance that I bypassed the big bucks by not reaching for the one-cent coins when only the Lincoln Memorial was visible. But any profits would have been negated by the scuffed up shoes and the holes in the pockets that would have been used as piggy banks.

For a measure of good fortune, I have searched for four leaf clovers, pulled on greasy wishbones, and reluctantly eaten cabbage on New Year's Day. If reminded, I might not walk under ladders, and I definitely do not open umbrellas in the house or sit around breaking mirrors.

Most days I could care less, but somewhere in the back of my mind a little voice tests me. "What do you have to lose? What if this is the one time in the history of the world that Lady Luck is handing you the key to prosperity? Go ahead. Believe in the good-luck charms. Pick up that penny." That "what if" can be a motivator.

Now I put dreams in the what-if category too. Are they messages from beyond, divine guidance, or did I leave the television on and absorbed some strange plots during the night? Actually we only had one TV when I was a kid, and the screen turned white at midnight. After the playing of the *National Anthem,* static filled the air waves until the a.m. news broke the silence.

Personally, I would not mind having a good story when the alarm goes off, but I rarely remember what goes on in my head at night. When I was a youngster, there was one big exception, a reoccurring dream. In it an Indian chief had set up a teepee in Grandpa's pasture.

For whatever reasons, the cavalry and the Petty boys got rid of him before dawn. It seemed so unbelievably real that I checked the pasture the next day. Hoof prints and possible signs of buffalo were everywhere. Sure, my cousins assumed that Dolly the horse and her sidekick, the milk cow, had been walking near the creek. If I had been with the people who attacked that magnificent warrior, I might have said the same thing.

The dreams that tend to fill me with an overwhelming sense of foreboding are Julie's. She has a real talent for imagination when her eyes are shut. It might not surprise you, but occasionally I am the villain in some of her slumber plots.

It amazes me that she can hold on to a grudge all day long after the Sandman has visited. When the imaginary me is in one of her visions and upsets her, the real me suffers significantly harsh looks until she sorts out the fiction from the facts. A lot of times I stay in the dog house until she finally puts her finger on something that I am truly guilty of.

Since Julie and I were married, I can only recall having one powerful dream. It occurred months after our daughter April died. In it I responded to a late-night knock, and April burst in when the door was opened. She laughed and kissed my forehead, and hugged the daylights out of me. Then we moved to the living room. (Living room? Mr. Irony just can't stay away, can he?)

That crazy girl plopped down on my lap, waved wildly at Julie, and could not wait to tell us that she was happy. The voice and the rhythm and the vocabulary were hers. Even in my sleep, I could feel my heart pounding and tears trickling down my face.

When April stood up to race to her mother, she stumbled on the carpet and somersaulted to her feet. She giggled and interjected, "I haven't gotten used to my new legs yet." Hers had been broken when she fell from an apartment window. She had lived only a week after the accident.

I woke up and wiped my face on the pillow cover. Wishfully and quietly I shuffled to the living room and opened the front door. If she had been standing there, I would have let her in and pretended that she had never died. Instead I slumped on the couch and cried when I did not find her.

Superstitions and messages from the beyond do not determine my tomorrows, but I'd like to think that there are special moments that any of us can choose to believe in. My heart accepts her visit and the conversation as one of my What Ifs.

When the Right Words Seem Wrong

Far too often, I pick up the paper to find that another young person has died. We are a big enough community but also a small enough place. I do not know everyone, but I know so many. Sometimes I am friends with the child or the child's family.

Talking to anyone who has lost a son or daughter is difficult. Do they really want or need to discuss anything? It has been eighteen years, and I might still get emotional if I try to speak about April. I can look at pictures now and even share a memory or two; but, if someone looks into my eyes and asks me how I am dealing with it, I may lose my voice and almost cry.

Weeks after a child's funeral, I have sometimes mailed a letter to the family. It was unedited and rambled on forever, but the content captured years of thoughts about grief and loss. I wanted the family to know that they were not alone and tried to put on paper what I could not say aloud.

It was difficult to type with tears blurring my vision, but eventually the letter would be stamped and mailed. Only in the last year or so did I find the strength to revise it. When I did, it was easy to see that I had thought too long, written too much, and tried too hard to say what can't necessarily be said. It was just as obvious that I was talking to myself.

Here is the most recent letter:

Dear Friend,
   You may not have known our April, but I think you would have loved her. She

was beautiful. (Thank God, my girls look like Julie!) She wanted to be a teacher and have five kids. She sang like an angel and was a karaoke queen. April died a week before her nineteenth birthday.

In the past when a teacher or friend has lost a child, I tried to write something meaningful to them. Yet somewhere between "it hurts to think about it" and "what do I possibly have to say" I found a reason to erase the letter and shut off the computer. Finally I decided that I would not let that happen. I typed and hoped that the thoughts would never need to be sent.

I visit April's grave all the time. After the funeral, I felt compelled to light a candle every evening and drove from Columbus to Azalia to do that. When bad weather prevented the trip, I discovered that my dad or sister were somehow getting to the cemetery and lighting one for her and for me.

We lit a candle daily for the first three years after she died. It was my need, maybe my dad's, but probably not hers. A favorite April memory was when she sang the solo part of "This Little Light of Mine" at a middle school concert. I wanted her to have her own little light forever. For the last fourteen years, a solar light has been at the grave. I didn't want my family getting out in bad weather any more.

Is there a point to all that? Yes. We won't forget our kids. They are with us, and so are those who try to take care of us. I know it is difficult for you and for all your family. It will always be difficult. It has been seventeen years since our April died. Things are different now, but for me they are still hard at times.

Six months after her funeral, people would ask, "Is it better?" They said a lot of things that didn't always make sense – probably because they didn't know what to say. They hoped that we had finished the grief cycle in eight weeks and were at peace. It rarely works that way. Love has great rewards and great costs. Life is about cherishing the rewards and enduring the costs and about growing from both.

In the months that followed April's death, there was an article in the Louisville Courier *that caught my attention. The initial statement was something like:*

> Grief is the unwelcome visitor who stands at the front door long after the other guests have gone.

We don't just get through grief in a few months. We face it one day at a time. It can be a powerful presence for three to five years ... and sometimes longer. Our hearts hurt as we learn to face the day and take care of our families.

Shopping was a nightmare that first year. I would get groceries after midnight so everyone wouldn't "stare" at me. No, they weren't really staring, but I felt that I had a big sign on me that said, "This guy lost his daughter. This guy couldn't pray enough to help his own child." Sometimes I cried in the aisles where her favorite snacks were shelved. I hated tears in public places, but I could feel them coming at the oddest times ... like when I spotted a box of crackers that she liked.

It was five years before I could enter the room that had been April's without collapsing. When no one was home, I would sneak in for a moment to look for treasures and miracles. I wanted to see her or to spot a piece of paper with her handwriting. I especially needed to hear her voice and laughter. But instead, I found myself on the floor because I did not have the strength to stand.

Sometimes I think about things that must have been contemplated for centuries.

1. *Why do people pray from their knees? When I collapsed in April's room, I was so hurt, so alone, and so helpless. I didn't have the strength to stand. Isn't it too bad that it took such a harsh event like that to motivate me to seek help from God and from my friends? I would bet that throughout the ages other people have faced similar experiences. At that point, they may have asked for strength and guidance and learned to pray.*

2. *Why do we think heaven is above us? When I would search for April, I couldn't find her in the room or house. But, on a clear day I could see her*

face in the sky. When I looked away from the busy streets, from the task at hand, from all the people.... When I looked up, I could put her image in the clouds. It was comforting to think she was in heaven and that she might be watching. Maybe I am the only one who does that.

3. *Is it okay to be mad at God? I don't ask for permission, but I think that God has broad shoulders. Sometimes I get angry. I want a WHY, a reason for the tragedy. God knows when I am mad because I tell Him. Most of us show our anger with people we trust, with people we know will love us unconditionally. So, who better to dump on than God? He gave us those emotions and knows we will use them.*

4. *Why do we think the heart is the center of emotion? On days when the grief is the heaviest, it feels like there is a hole in my chest where my heart should be. It is a huge emptiness.*

One of the biggest problems I still face is that I don't want anyone to forget her. On the other hand, I don't want anyone to catch me off guard by mentioning her when I am not ready for the discussion. Yes, I want people to talk about her. I want to hear a song that she loved to sing. And, I want to think that friends and family still cherish her memory. But, if someone surprises me with a story, my emotions may show. I hate not having that control.

Another irony is that even though April is not with me, she is with me all the time. In the first year, there was not a moment that she might not be on my mind. She was the first thing I thought about when I woke up, the last thing on my heart when I fell asleep, and often a beautiful, distracting presence throughout the day.

I had to work on that, and you might have to work on it. I constantly reminded myself that I loved other people too, but it was not easy to focus on them. It sounds silly, but I ended up making a mobile scrapbook. I could see April's face in the sky, but I needed to see the rest of my family too.

So, I found pictures of everyone else and made twenty copies of each. I put them in my tool box, in the glove compartment and trunk of my car, on my shaving mirror, and lots of other places. I couldn't open a sock drawer without seeing a picture and saying to myself, "Have you spent any time talking with your other girls today?" And, if someone made me mad, that person's picture went in the underwear drawer.

Because I wanted to be in control, I made a lot of "never promises" during those first few years. I was never going to let bad things happen again to someone I loved. I was never going to get angry over the little things. In a way, I think I promised I was never going to be human or to allow those I loved to learn and grow from their experiences.

These days I try to limit the never promises. I was smothering myself and others with a lot of good intentions and the pretense that if the rules were followed, a safety net would pop up over my family. That can happen, but we don't control all the factors, do we?

The biggest promise I try to keep now is that at the end of the day, I want to have said what I needed to say, have done what I could, and have unconditionally loved ... not necessarily coddled or enabled ... those who are a part of my life. I don't want to live each day as if it is my last. I want to live each day as if I have done what needs to be done for those I am with.

I still read about grief because I still feel the effects. But, these days I don't hide from it as much as I first did. It may not get better, but it is much different now. I am able to celebrate her life again.

I know that you miss (your child) and that (he/she) is as wonderful and caring as ours. You and your family are in my thoughts and prayers.

Accepting April's death and coming to terms with all the emotions has taken years. The process remains a work-in-progress. Putting the thoughts on paper was not easy. It really was too much to have shared, but writing the letter lifted a burden from me. The postage did not cover the weight of the content.

The Sting

The storm buried the driveway and closed the schools, and my personal castle was under attack. Doubting that everyone in our household would be excused from work, I shut off the alarm and just lay in bed for a while. Where had I put the winter boots and my shoveling clothes? The insulated coveralls would keep me warm enough once I started moving.

Finally awake, I opened a diet coke and put a couple of slices of bread in the toaster. We had butter, but no one ever put it back in the fridge in the same place. By the time the white bread was brown I had turned on the news and cleared a spot at the table. A primeval nature lets the protector of the land awaken early and grumble silently about his breakfast if he has to waste time looking for the margarine.

When I finished second guessing where the butter should have been stored, I found the blue coveralls in the corner of the garage. The orange lining made them easy to spot. Tilting the ladder provided enough space to catch hold of the collar and to lift them off the nail. I balanced against the side of the van and shoved a leg through. There was nothing graceful about squeezing arms and legs into the suit and zipping it up.

I paused for a moment and regretted that I had not straightened up the garage in the fall, but I generally found what I was searching for. Years of justifying my faults allowed me to be pleased that there was order in my disorder. Why couldn't the girls emulate my gift when they worked in the kitchen?

Once I had the gloves on and the shovel in hand, there was no excuse. Armed for battle, I raised the garage door and stepped out to face the challenge. Yet after only two steps, I dropped the shovel, shouted "Ouch" to the gods, and danced around as I stripped off the top of the coveralls.

There was no tightness in the chest and no spreading discomfort, but the pain was sudden and intense. A jabbing, hot sting brought a wince and a childish cry. Something had bitten me. Simultaneously I countered with rapid slaps to my right shoulder and ripped at the zipper. A dead yellow jacket fell in the snow when I tugged out my arm.

Bees and wasps had been on the attack all summer long. Even in the shade, I had worn a hat for protection as they lay siege. The cap protected my head and substituted as a flyswatter when they got too close. At some point, the fierce predators must have gathered at the library, read *The Iliad*, and planned this Homeric subterfuge. Instead of the Trojan Horse, they would use Larry's Coveralls. Only the bravest of the brave would be selected to sneak inside the heavy, one-piece garment and await the enemy.

Clearing the drive took two hours that morning. In the beginning my frosty breath was more evident than my progress, but eventually a path was forged. The job allowed ample time for questions. Did my body heat wake up the yellow jacket? How many people get stung while they are shoveling snow? Did I need a tetanus shot?

The summer confrontation with the bees had been forgotten, but it reemerged with a vengeance. How often in life will the events and adversaries of seasons past come back to bite me?

Nudge Me Gently

Towards the Wrinkles

Grandpa Petty

"Just remember, when you're over the hill, you begin to pick up speed."

Charles M. Schulz

Simple Genetics

Grandpa looked like Grandpa. I don't know that I could describe him for an artist; but if he was in a lineup with all the men who ever lived in Clark County, I could pick him out with one eye shut.

He was not a big man, but he was big enough. He butchered hogs and hunted rabbits and milked the cow and held down a job and farmed. How do you measure that in inches and pounds?

Sometimes I stared at his nails. Instead of curving smoothly across the end of his fingers, they were creased like the brim of a ball cap that had been bent and folded. Some were yellowed from holding an unfiltered cigarette until it was too small to be held.

But, his eyes are what I remember most. They looked tired. They were framed by weathered wrinkles that stretched across his face. Puffy bags hung beneath them and arched like the rims of glasses. Grandpa died when I was a teenager, but his eyes still visit.

I can't tell you how many times I have casually remarked to a friend, "You look more like your dad every time I see you." Cousin Rick does. Cousin Ronnie might, and my friend Bill is starting too.

When I said it to Jim, he was quick to respond, "I see him every morning when I shave."

Sometimes I visit a newborn and listen to the crowd debate which parent or grandparent the baby resembles. For the life of me, I can't do that. Oh, I might say it but only because it seems to please people that the world will be re-blessed with such a wonderful image.

My preference is to wait four or five decades before making such astute observations and remarking, "You sure look like your mom or your dad." Better yet, I'd rather let the individual decide whose gene pool is responsible for the image.

Physically I am a lot more Petty than Perkinson. Yet I don't exactly look like any one member of the family except when I glance in the rear view mirror and see familiar eyes that are surrounded by wrinkles and have the bags beneath them.

Occasionally that moment lets me greet Grandpa with a smile and reflect, "I remember you. We met years ago."*

*"*I remember you*" is such a common statement, but after reading Ray Bradbury's *Remembrance*, the English teacher in me feels that Bradbury owns the line. I invite you to read the poem but have no regrets that I use the sentence on a regular basis.

May the Cure

None of us want to get sick, but we know it can happen so unexpectedly. According to my interpretation of the myth, an army of germs flew out when Pandora's Box was opened; and those forces have been preying on mankind ever since. Fortunately a lot of smart people are always finding antidotes for some of the ailments that escaped; but, to this day, "May the cure not be worse that the disease" offers sound wisdom.

My friend Bob never benefited much from getting ill when he was a boy, so playing hooky was out of the question. If he was too sick for school, he was too sick to walk to the outhouse. His older sister made it painfully clear that he would have to use the bedpan should a need arise. I'd say that Bob developed a healthy fear of the metal receptacle and of his sister.

Personally, the marketable balms of Gilead, namely Vicks Salve, horrified me. When the sneezing, wheezing effects of the common cold whipped me good -- when my eyes couldn't open and my nose was painfully red -- when my temperature rose and breathing became difficult, the smell of the vapor rub was heavy in the air. It was then that I learned that a body may have to get worse before it gets better.

My mother accepted the medical practitioner's duties as a calling. Dr. Teal might see us once in a while, but it would not be for a runny nose. Money could not buy a pill or procedure that was better than the thick, gooey substance that could be purchased at any store that truly cared about children. If there is a correlation between odor and success, the Vick's ointment was worth the money.

The instructions were unwritten but clear:

"For best results, have your child smear the product all over the chest area. Indirectly this allows for a substantial amount to plug up the nostrils since kids will certainly rub their noses before cleaning their hands. Then coat an inch layer of the stinky mess to a handkerchief or sock and place it around the loved one's neck. Leave some space, but tie the medicated poultice so that it can never be removed. Remember: this is not a tourniquet."

No wonder I worried about home remedies in those days and am skeptical now of recommended cures. Recently new concerns awaked when I battled flu symptoms for a week before being sidelined by gout. It had been over a year since the last gout attack, and I had hoped it would never occur again. The touch of the sheet against my big toe made sleeping impossible, and my soft, new slippers were all I could get on. I was a little self-conscious that they did not match any of my dress pants.

Like Popeye, who said, "That's all I can stands. I can't stands no more," I decided to take action. Therefore, I made an appointment with the doctor. Besides, visiting for two afflictions seemed to be a money-saving move. Maybe I should have just opened a can of spinach or a jar of Vicks.

Surprisingly, the office wait was short. Within ten minutes of checking in at the front desk, I was escorted from the waiting room and telling the nurse about my problems. The only delay in the diagnosis was at the let's–weigh-the-big-guy scales. I tried to bypass the apparatus, but the wily young lady would have none of it. Apparently the doctor could not heal my conditions unless he matched the dosage to my weight.

Lots of questions later, it appeared that getting better would require more than chicken soup and rest. Antibodies could address the cold symptoms, but gout is a tremendously mean-spirited, stubborn enemy that only a mercenary force can eliminate. That was evident when I had to get a loan for the bottle of prescribed pills that would battle the maladies. Despite the doctor's assurances of a quick recovery, I remained an unbeliever and a poorer one at that after visiting the pharmacy.

Does anyone besides me ever really read the information that come with the medicine bottles? Past experiences have proven that I am susceptible to every listed side effect, so I feel obligated to skim through my future before leaving the parking lot. This time the tell-my-fortune sheet stated that the medicinal product "may loosen stool." I had never seen that one before but was impressed that they used the word *stool*. My brother Gene would have summarized it differently.

Well, the morning after, I am here to tell you that "loosen stool" is not a side-effect. It is a dire warning from the ancient oracles that may not yet have a modern translation. Here is as close as I can get:

> "Beware. If you swallow this tiny blue tablet, you won't worry about the gout at all. Instead, you will fear the loss of

whatever dignity you have left in life. Any sneeze, stumble, bump, or change in temperature may result in your soiling yourself."

Additionally, if you still have that nagging cough when this affliction cripples you, you might as well pull out the Sears and Roebuck catalog. You'll need to purchase a new mattress and sheets as soon as your foot is well enough to allow you to drive to the post office and put the order form in the mail.

Officially Older

Birthday candles are not the only reminders of my age. The AARP membership offers have increased, and today I received a letter asking me to invest in a mail-order cremation plan. The depressing ad was tossed on a pile that will sit and collect dust, but not my dust.

Last week I regretfully accepted that I was officially ready to order from the senior menu. The epiphany occurred when I nudged Julie and pointed at a young couple with kids. The words had escaped too easily, and there was no taking them back.

"Remember when we were that young?"

Two little blondes stood in the grocery cart. A third held her father's hand and was tugging him toward the impulse items that were stacked near the register. How many times did I dread that a similar, tiny hand had picked up an item that I did not have the money for?

Their family dynamics made me smile, and I need to get better at that. I work on it daily because my social filter is clogging up. At my age, groaning and frowning increase with each birthday. I used to receive presents, but now I just get the gift of grumpiness after I blow out the rows of candles. Even when there is no discomfort, moaning and complaining about the little things go together like mustard and ketchup on a burger.

These days a mild gasp greets the weekly posting of food and fuel prices. And heaven help the person who has the audacity to be looking for the same can of peaches that I came to shop for. You can't blame a guy for verbalizing his annoyance when the only two people in the entire store want the same product, especially when that other person gets there first. If the peach thief reaches for glasses, you might as well give a double moan. Watching him read the label about nutritional facts before he steals the fruit only prolongs the misery.

Social groaning and huffing are partners; but as long as you aren't caught rolling your eyes, you can probably get away with either one. Before the accuser can challenge your lack of good social skills, put a hand on a knee or shoulder and pretend to massage the ache away. Make sure you grimace a little. Since it is difficult to distinguish between pain and grumpiness, most people will not call you out for bad manners if they believe that soreness, not surliness, is possibly the culprit.

Maybe I shouldn't be allowed to pick up groceries without Julie there to supervise me; but if I do, it wouldn't hurt to wander the aisles and gather inspiration from the families who are enjoying each other's company. While I am at it, I might even shop for a better attitude and hope that I can't afford to bypass the bargain.

Being an older adult and enjoying each day is a challenge, but it is an option that I hope to pursue. Most of us need to smile more often. There is enough wailing and gnashing of teeth in this world. If anguish persists, let the body release what it can but avoid wasting energy on the little battles in life. Participating in the activities that make us feel young and alive will help us be more positive.

If I ever decide to buy into that cremation plan, I would like my grin to be so regular that the undertaker sees it when he lights the funeral pyre. That will take some practice on my part.

The Lost Scrolls

I found an old box hidden on a basement shelf under some "I once thought this was important" debris. The weight of the dust and the delicate cobwebs secured the lid. When I removed the cover, the cardboard sides buckled enough to reveal paperwork that had been buried for a long time.

After college, I had stored many a dog-eared text for a decade or more. Some were for reference, and some reminded me of a particular assignment that I had enjoyed. A number of them were from Dr. England's classes at Indiana State.

I also kept research papers, some creative pieces, and an essay or two. A few of each were in the box. I paused and read for a while. It amused me that they were handwritten. I would imagine that only typed assignments are acceptable today. Many a night had been spent writing and rewriting until the final copy was free of mistakes and soda stains.

Reading the yellowed pages was uncomfortable. The topics must have had purpose back then. An understanding of how history impacts writers came with one class. Early American literature was an obvious favorite. I had enjoyed the long hours at the library and the late-night process of piecing together insight from ten to twenty sources. The discomfort did not come from the memories of labor. It came because I recognized the penmanship but not the author.

The reading voice in my head stumbled through the pages. Since I was not hearing me,

I tried another paper. No, I did not know that person either.

The writer had put on his bench-press gloves and hoisted huge words from the thesaurus. He had borrowed the voices of the author's whom he had quoted. None of it was plagiarized, but the style was mimicked. He had captured ideas and put them on paper. He had polished research skills, improved vocabulary, and somehow survived a world without spell check. He had debated truths, analyzed characters, and sought the meaning of life.

These days when someone gives me a book, I read a chapter or two, set the book aside, and return to it in a week. I am not debating whether I like it or not. I am introducing myself to the author's style and voice. I want to know who is talking to me. Later, when I am ready to spend more time, I find that the initial meet-and-greet has benefits. I am a better reader and listener if I feel acquainted. Visiting the first chapter helps.

Most of the essays in that old box recorded my research voice, one that I no longer practice and one that may have been the cure for insomnia. I am sure that I have other styles, both auditory and written. Among them are the voices for daughters and granddaughters and "ah-oh, I'm in trouble." There must be ones for "Julie, can you find my ...," for frustration, and for "I am so grateful." There is a silent one that screams within when emotions overwhelm me and I cannot express what I am feeling.

Which voices do I use to meet and greet? Which ones invite someone back even when the conversation feels uncomfortable? Which voice asks for forgiveness?

We lose some things during our lives, and we find some things. Obviously the contents of that crumbling container were in no way comparable to the Dead Sea Scrolls. The only revelation that was hidden beneath the dust was that I have gone in a different direction. I have changed.

Phantom Moments

"Hurry. Get up. Be quick, or you'll miss these cute little boys with the long hair." My mom rapped sharply on the headboard as she spoke.

Some unacceptable conduct had interfered with our evening privileges, but I do not remember what my siblings had done. Regardless, we had been sent to bed early. Yet, to our delight, an unexpected reprieve had been granted

"You'd better get moving," she encouraged before heading back to the living room. It was obvious that she had no intentions of missing the performance.

It would have been horrible to have been the only kids at school the next day who had not watched the Beatles on *The Ed Sullivan Show* that Sunday night. For at least an evening, my mother thought they were adorable. In the weeks to follow, however, it became very clear that what was okay for the lads from Liverpool was not as acceptable for the boys who resided with Lester and Lillie Perkinson. More than once we were told that there would be no long hair.

I have often debated if the emphatic "NO LONG HAIR" was a command or prophecy. Our dining room doubled as a barbershop for years, and Mom did not accept requests or payment. Short on the sides and enough to comb over on top pretty much described what was left when the clippers were put away. By the time I could sit down and discuss alternative styles with a professional barber, I had the permanent Friar Tuck look.

Now I do have a little hair, and it still remains short on the sides. If I wake up and find that the bed hair frightens me when I look in the mirror, it is time for a trim. I try to get it wet enough to lie down and hope that I am not mistaken for one of the Three Stooges when I drive to Wingler's barbershop.

Amazingly, my hair grows twice as fast on the left side. I wonder if Sampson had that happen. If so, I imagine that he battled the Philistines ambidextrously. With the jawbone of an ass he would have killed three thousand with the right hand and seven thousand with the left. His enemies would have warned their children, "Stay close to home. The Southpaw of Death could be nearby."

For "one brief, shining moment" my hair had been parted in JFK fashion, but for most of my life I have been bald. Once in a while I forget that the blonde strands are gone. When I do, blind fingers reach up and push the phantom locks to the right even though they disappeared when I was in my twenties.

If a man can forget that his hair is gone, what else can the years rob him of? It's hard not to feel old some days, but most of us just don't give up on our youth so easily. Oh, we may complain and slow down, but in our hearts we yearn for another adventure. Hopefully we try to engage the day one more time no matter how many birthdays we've had. Our bodies may be older, but our spirits don't have to get wrinkled.

Tomorrow I may have to show off my own youthful spirit. I plan to brush that mop of non-existent hair right out of my eyes, listen to a Beatles' song, and talk with Julie when the alarm goes off. And, if she gives me a hug and hints that it might be time for a haircut, I'll gladly sign in at the barbershop and read a magazine until one of the Winglers calls my name.

Gleaning Time

Fortunately the temperature stayed warm enough to prevent the snow and ice that had been in the forecast. So, instead of massive drifts or a soft, smooth blanket of white, the landscape was gray and brown and corn-row rough. But, these were not barren fields. They were just empty.

Before the arrival of the combines, last year's crops -- like the crops before them -- had hidden the immensity of the land and blocked the view of the houses and buildings that were now so evident. Soon enough, plowing and planting would start again, along with an apprehension that the work might not be rewarded.

The seasonal, morning haze masked the blemishes of aging farms, but little scrutiny was needed to spot the wear and tear of time. Rusty silo roofs showed their years. A missing board and a broken pane were evident but hardly diminished the worth of the storage structures. Old equipment remained buried in the belly of the monstrous weeds of summer that had swallowed them.

On both sides of the highway, corn stubble lined the fields. The pale yellow remnants of harvest rose a half foot at most above the soil. Some stood straight, but others no longer pointed to the sky as they had done when they reached for the warmth of the summer sun.

To my right, faint straw-colored stalks stretched out in long lines. It would be months before the wheat would be seen and more months before anyone looked at amber waves of grain. For now, the only signs of life were the scavengers.

The crows gleaned a land that other animals had pilfered for months. Fields that had once seemed rich now offered almost nothing for the black birds that pillaged the soil and waited for the chance to rob each other if any food were found. Occasionally one took flight as if sailing a few feet above the ground might reveal whole ears of corn. Yet no such treasures were left.

Would a foot of snow have canceled their gathering, or would the crows have just looked elsewhere? I don't know enough about them to speculate. My knowledge of birds peaked in elementary school. We were the Azalia Cardinals. In fact, if ball-game chants be true, we were the "mighty, mighty Cardinals." Maybe redbirds are more welcomed at bird feeders and sanctuaries. Unlike the crows, they might not need to fight for food in a winter wasteland.

The first graders at Azalia were tagged with a number wildlife names in reading class. Some of us were probably redbirds. I don't recall what species Mrs. Jones chose to represent the good readers or which she used to denote those who needed extra help. It could have been sparrows or robins or foxes. What I am certain of is that some of us should have been squirrels. We fidgeted in our seats far too much to concentrate on vowels and consonants and silent letters.

If Mrs. Jones asked me to pick my own group today, I would excuse myself from the list of foxes and squirrels. And, I don't believe I qualify as a robin or sparrow either. These days I feel more akin to the old crows that extracted kernels from a greedy, muddy land. Like them I search continuously when I am hungry and empty, but I dig through mounds and fields of memories to meet a portion of my needs.

In an effort to reclaim what was lost we sort through our experiences again and again, and sometimes we just stumble across one accidently. What we discover can affect our attitudes and our tomorrows. The desire to look for value in our lives and the hope that comes from finding something special, nudge us gently through the day and into the next season.

About the Author

Larry Perkinson has four beautiful daughters, Julie – a remarkably understanding wife, and two wonderful granddaughters.

After graduating from Indiana State in 1975, he taught middle school English in North Vernon, Indiana. Four years later he moved to the Bartholomew Consolidated School Corporation in Columbus. In 1996, he accepted a teaching position that allows him to work with students, families, and the community to develop an understanding of obstacles and supports that are related to student learning and relationships. He coached football for five years, track for ten, and wrestling for thirty one.

He is a member of the Sandcreek-Azalia Friends Meeting House.

Larry's first book, *Daffodils and Dog-ears*, shares personal experiences and life markers. The stories will rekindle your own memories. You will find love, laughter, and a bit of self-compassion as you visit with him and get reacquainted with yourself.

Made in USA - North Chelmsford, MA
1114416_9781512097023
05.21.2020 1309